1126 00095 1026

2-16-84

D1217705

# KATHY BOUDIN

## AND THE

# DANCE OF DEATH

# KATHY BOUDIN

## AND THE

# DANCE OF DEATH

## Ellen Frankfort

STEIN AND DAY/*Publishers*/New York

First published in 1983
Copyright © 1983 by Ellen Frankfort
All rights reserved, Stein and Day, Incorporated
Designed by Louis A. Ditizio
Printed in the United States of America
STEIN AND DAY/*Publishers*
Scarborough House
Briarcliff Manor, N.Y. 10510

**Library of Congress Cataloging in Publication Data**

Frankfort, Ellen.
  Kathy Boudin and the dance of death.

  1. Boudin, Kathy.  2. Female offenders—United States—
Biography.  3. Weather Underground Organization.
I. Title.
HV6248.B665F7  1983      364.1'092'4  [B]      83-40082
ISBN 0-8128-2946-8

To Rolise
and the women
of the country compound

# CONTENTS

# KATHY BOUDIN
# AND THE
# DANCE OF DEATH

# PART ONE

# *ACTION*

# 1

# THE BIG DANCE

KATHY Boudin met Michael Koch at the point of a gun. The off-duty correction officer was driving north on the New York State Thruway when he noticed the flashing lights at an entrance to the opposite side a short distance away. He stopped his van to check it out. It looked like some kind of roadblock.

Within seconds he saw a black cop go down, a wild shootout, and a woman scrambling down the cliffrock to the Thruway, away from the gunfire. Once on the road, she started to run as if she were fleeing for her life.

Where was she going? Good or bad, he wanted her.

He bounded out of the van, drew his gun and badge, raced across six lanes, and caught her at the underpass.

"Freeze! Don't move! Police officer!"

Dark hair, slight build, wide and frightened eyes. Out of breath. Hands held half up at eye level. Staring at the gun.

She was saying over and over, through ragged breath, "I didn't shoot him! He did! He shot him! I didn't shoot him! Don't shoot me! Please don't let them hurt me!"

Gun drawn, he frisked her. No weapon. Damn, he didn't have any cuffs either. He pulled her leather coat down to bind her arms, using her as a shield as he moved up toward the black cop on the ground.

A wounded detective was giving the cop mouth-to-mouth.

"Do you have any handcuffs?"

The detective stopped, looked up, stared a second at the bearded man with the woman in his grip.

"Holy shit, it's her."

He jumped up, pushed the woman to the ground, face down, and handcuffed her.

The trembling woman, her head on broken glass, stared at her captor who had taken the detective's place. She saw his mouth meet the open mouth of the mortally wounded officer and the fountain of blood flowing from the black man's body.

Kathy Boudin was no longer Underground.

Someone would have to tell Leonard Boudin about his daughter, Kathy. It was tricky; Leonard had a pacemaker and a history of heart trouble. But there was no way to shield him from the news. Still, it was unpleasant to disturb the stillness of his home, nested in its cozy little enclave.

If city streets could be metaphors for the way people live, the Boudins' would be perfect. The eastern end starts out with some old tenementlike buildings, railroad-flat walkups inhabited mainly by not-yet-successful artists who are new to Greenwich Village. The block then takes a surprise curve; suddenly one sees a row of perfect, Victorian-styled brownstones, right down to the gaslights. It is one of the few blocks in Manhattan lined with gingko trees. The houses, with their floor-to-ceiling parlor windows, wrought-iron grillwork and old oak doors, are saved from a thoroughbred elegance by the public playground across the street. That also allows the southern light to stream through the parlor floors and enhance the growth of the plants that hang from the high ceilings.

At its western end, the block becomes somewhat raunchy as it juts out into a warehouse section, near the Hudson River, currently being converted to posh housing. Only recently,

14

solar collectors appeared on the roof of a mammoth building, and a former printing factory became "Printing House."

A few blocks from the Boudin brownstone is the Old Federal Jail, where Robert Lowell once spent time for antiwar activities. It is now a fancy co-op. The Metropolitan Correction Center, where Kathy would spend time, has replaced it.

As soon as Leonard found out about his daughter's arrest, he wasted no time getting on the phone. There was only one thing on his mind: his daughter was being charged with murder. Now he would have to convince everyone of her innocence.

Leonard put his hand through his long silvery hair as he waited for an answer. Although not necessarily his choice for the permanent counsel, Bill Kunstler would be fine for the moment. Shortly after Leonard called, Bill was on his way to Nyack.

What bothered Leonard was Kathy's reported remark, "I didn't shoot him. He did." Even a lawyer less brilliant than Boudin would recognize it as a possible acknowledgment that she knew what was going on. Well, this was all the more reason to start thinking of the sharpest legal minds—which colleagues had earned their reputations by brilliant, and preferably cool, understated performances. Leonard understood that it was he who would have to orchestrate it all. He had said, in the past, "I do not lose cases." This was going to be a tough one. But it was also the most important. This was his daughter.

Kunstler arrived just as Kathy was being taken from the Rockland County jail into the Nyack Police Station. Although the lights from the TV crews made it feel more like a Broadway opening than an arraignment, the sight of his friend's daughter in handcuffs was heartbreaking; for the moment Kunstler didn't know for whom he felt the greater compassion—Leonard or Kathy. He looked at his watch. Not quite midnight. Leonard would be pleased; he had gotten up there quickly.

Eight hours earlier, the Brink's silver-and-white armored truck had lumbered on its way.

A perfect fall day, a choice route up the Palisades, twenty-five banks to stop at. No sweat.

Close to four o'clock the armored truck moved along the ramp to the upper level of the windowless, charcoal-brick Nanuet Mall. Crawling past acres of parked cars, it pulled up to an entrance. The only sign, far to the left of the door, was a metal plaque: Nanuet National/Irving Bank Corp.

Kelly, the driver, parked so the side door of the truck would receive the cash. Paige, the guard, took his position in front of the truck. He stood against the wall. That way, he could see when Trombino, the messenger, came out of the mall and could shield him until he got back inside the truck with the sacks of money. Twenty-four years of practice. Ten minutes, in and out.

The driver got ready to hit the button that opened the door to the storage compartment.

A red Chevy van pulled up just as Trombino emerged from the bank, pushing a cart with canvas sacks. Kelly had his finger on the button when it happened. Three loud noises. Gunfire? He saw Paige grimace in pain. He let go of the button, drew his gun, and looked around to see where the shots came from. From the cab he couldn't see the three men in ski masks jump out of the van.

One, pistol in hand, raced toward the shoppers leaving the mall and kept them at bay. A second gunman ran up to Paige, pointed his automatic pistol, and, without warning, fired into his throat. Paige went down. Another burst in the thigh. Paige died face down on the sidewalk.

Now Kelly could see two men in masks. Each had a gun;

one stationed himself behind the van and the other in front. Kelly raised his head a bit to look for Paige. The gunman in front turned toward the truck. He looked straight at the windshield, took dead aim, and fired. Kelly tried to duck, but he hit his head as he landed on the floor. Showered by shattered window hail, he felt something pierce him behind the left ear. He struggled to raise himself and reached the button for the door.

Everything was a blur. A five-man construction crew scampered down the scaffolding. People ducked for cover, crouched under cars, behind fenders. Kelly saw Trombino racing toward the truck with the handcart and pressed the button to open the door and let him in. Again he heard gunfire. One, two shots. Trombino, who had just managed to step into the truck, was trying to close the door when the bullets hit him in the arm. His arm looked to Kelly like a piece of meat that had just been cut.

Kelly took aim through the gun-port as the gunman came running by. He managed to get a shot before he slumped to the floor of the truck.

It was a particularly bloody bank job. One dead, one severely wounded, and $1.6 million gone.

The Big Dance. They had pulled it off. They took all six bags out of the Brink's truck and put them in the van, pulled out of the mall, and sped down 59. Left behind were Beefsteak Charlie's, Video Arcade, Herman's Sporting World, Computer Center, and the other stores of the Nanuet Mall.

Ahead lay their goal, just past McDonald's, Jack LaLanne, Pathmark, Toy and Sports Warehouse.

Ahead lay Korvette's, a dead discount center, an empty parking lot in the rear. It was a quiet place to rendezvous with a Honda with Jersey plates and a U-Haul truck from Nebraska.

And behind the lot were just trees, thinning in October.

17

The red van pulled up to Shipping and Receiving. The gunmen looked around, then gave a signal. The trunk of the Honda sprang open.

Some climbed with the green canvas sacks into the back of the U-Haul; others leapt into the Honda. Doors slammed as they sped off, leaving the red van behind, the motor running.

They drove east again, straight on Route 59, keeping an eye out for Kentucky Fried Chicken, then turned.

Sign on the right: "West Nyack Cares."

Sign on the right: "Central Nyack Cares."

The U-Haul pulled ahead of a car and waited in the left lane for the light at the intersection.

Five after four. Sirens.

The Big Dance hit a snag.

Roadblock at the Thruway.

The woman dialed the police. Her house was not the only one in the trees and bushes—there were others behind Korvette's. But she saw, through the thin October trees, and she called. Once the police answered, the words blurted out— guns, money bags, a U-Haul. Then she hung up and stared at the back of the defunct store: the electric power transformers, the air conditioning and heating units on top of the old building, and the big green dumpster. It was enough to give you the creeps. She went to check the lock on her door. She wasn't sure of the exact number of gunmen there had been, but it looked like seven, maybe eight.

Detective Keenan and Sergeant O'Grady, heading toward the Nanuet Mall, saw the U-Haul waiting to turn.

Officer Lennon drove up in another car. Keenan told him to block the ramp to the Thruway. When Lennon climbed out, he leveled the shotgun at the U-Haul.

The U-Haul came to a halt.

"Okay, miss. Open the door."

Kathy Boudin got out, her hands halfway up in the air. She looked very scared, nervous, jumpy.

They checked the cab—no weapons. A third car drove up, a black cop at the wheel.

"Keep an eye on her," the detective said to the black cop as the three of them walked to the back of the U-Haul.

"Please, what's wrong?" the woman asked as she stepped sideways across the road. "Can you put your gun away?"

"I don't think it's them. Put the gun away." Lennon listened to O'Grady and placed his shotgun in his car.

Detective Keenan tried the slide-down door. It held firm.

"I want to know what's in the back of the truck," he said.

The four moved away, then heard a noise in the truck.

The back crashed open. The detective turned. Men with guns jumped out.

One was shooting, automatic fire. The detective dove behind a tree, trying to get a good lead on him. A shot passed between Keenan's legs, almost hitting him.

The first shot had hit the black cop in the side. The impact raced up his back. Chipper Brown was lifted up and blown back.

Reloading, Keenan saw O'Grady hit.

Someone leapt back into the U-Haul and drove it into the police car barricade.

Kathy broke away from the blood, broken glass, gunfire, and started to climb down the rock leading to the Thruway.

Within seconds, several police cars converged, sirens wailing, lights flashing. In the confusion, three cars slipped away and zoomed north on Mountainview Avenue. South Nyack Police Chief Colsey noticed, leapt into his unmarked green car, and sped after them. Police at the scene flagged down an ambulance and placed Officer Brown next to a cardiac-arrest victim on his way to Nyack Hospital.

People whose cars were commandeered were left stranded at the roadblock. They were able to witness it all.

There was some confusion in the getaway cars. No one knew where Kathy was.

"Fuck it, man, forget her. They're on our ass. Step on it. Fast."

Up Mountainview—twisting, narrow, endless. "Slow, Children at Play." "15 MPH." Treacherous at 50. Lethal at 80.

"Shit, these curves, man. We gotta dump this car or we'll never get out of here." A driveway. Empty? "Yeah. Pull in." The commandeered BMW pulled in. The Honda and Olds screeched to a halt. Sam Brown, Judith Clark, and David Gilbert left in the Honda, Sam at the wheel; Marilyn Buck was driving the silver Olds.

They screeched back up the two-lane blacktop. Left, around, left, down. End of the road. Which way? East, man, then south. Turn right. Onto Christian Herald—no better than the other. The road slips around like a roller coaster. Up and down, up and down, and around. "Village Speed Limit 30." Merging with Old Mountain Road. Past Spook Hollow Road, Hudson View Road, a swerve right onto Midland Avenue. At last, a wide straightaway. More developed. People, too. Faster. Pick up speed. Past Birchwood, Castle Heights, Highmount, faster, south into the heart of Nyack.

"Fuck. A roadblock! Turn off!"

It wasn't a roadblock. The police cars, ambulances, lights, sirens, crowds were on Midland and Fifth to aid the wounded and try to save the dying.

The getaway drivers had swerved, swiveled, and sped to within a block of Nyack Hospital.

20

The Olds swung left, and up. And up. Sixth Avenue in Nyack. Perhaps the steepest hill in the village. Up, up, until the driver could glimpse the Hudson. Then down, down, hurtling toward the river. The '73 Olds braked, swung right onto Broadway, sped south past the Nyack police station, and Marilyn Buck had escaped.

"She made it! Now us. Watch it, man. Look out for that telephone pole."

Brown pole. Red firebox. Blue mailbox. Beige concrete wall. The chase was over. The Honda crashed into the wall at the house on the corner of Sixth Avenue and Broadway. They missed the home of Helen Hayes by a few feet.

The dazed three in the smashed Honda looked out the windows. The Honda tried, failed to start.

Passersby rushed up to help them.

"Stay back! Get away! They may be armed!" Chief Colsey had jumped out of his unmarked car and shouted through his bullhorn. "They're dangerous! Don't go near them!" The chief pulled out his gun. Within seconds he was joined by dozens of uniformed cops. Patrol cars crowded the crooked intersection.

Here they were at last. But who were they?

The driver, Sam Brown, a black man with a goatee, was lifted by three attendants onto a stretcher and into an ambulance.

David Gilbert, the white man, in his thirties, had a fuller beard. Long hair, too.

Judy Clark, slight with short, dark curly hair, was on the ground in seconds.

Clark and Gilbert were pulled up, pushed into patrol cars, and driven off.

"Let's keep it moving. Behind the barricades, please."

It was getting dark; the crowd broke off into small huddles, moving away from the site of the crash. The solid Queen Anne-style home, white with its black-tipped board and batten tower and sweeping veranda, looked magnificent in the reflected late-afternoon sun, its Victorian grace slightly marred by the crumpled metal heap at its steps.

Slowly, amid the buzz of whispers, there arose some talk of guns and murder. One small group moved in front of a porch covered with wisteria. Another stood by a house with pillars and an etched glass door.

"Lucky they missed the brick wall or they'd all be dead," someone murmured.

"Where'd they come from? I thought they were hippies or something."

"Not me. I knew they were no hippies. When I saw the white man with the beard and that hair—and those burning eyes. What came to my mind was Cult."

"Like Manson."

Light bulbs popped. Chief Colsey walked toward the trunk. The people on the street let out a gasp; a green canvas bag was lugged from the trunk of the car.

"I hope it's not another body," someone said.

"No, it's the money."

"What money?"

"Don't you know? They robbed a bank and shot some cops."

"Oh my God, I had no idea. I just thought it was a car crash."

"Anyone have Type O blood?" a cop called out, a radio close to his ear. A burly officer, gun in hand, buried his head on Chief Colsey's shoulder and sobbed.

All along North Broadway colored lights flickered through the large windows, some bay, some Palladian, some floor-to-ceiling; most of the lights came from TVs tuned to the evening news.

The plea for blood was repeated on the street.

"Why do they need blood? I thought the people who crashed were just shaken up."

"No, one guy was badly hurt. The driver."

"What do you mean, one guy? Haven't you heard? A group of gunmen shot and killed two cops."

"It wasn't gun*men*. There were women, too."

"Yes," he's right. I heard they caught one running on the Thruway."

"Who *is* she?"

"I don't know. But they say they're still around. Some are hiding out in the woods up in the hills. You should see it— helicopters flyin' around. They even set up a command post in the condos. You wouldn't believe it. It looks straight out of Vietnam."

Looking for fugitives near Mountain View Condominiums, Sierra Vista Lane, the 'copters invaded the prefab Swiss chalet village, their rotor blades rustling the windowbox geraniums.'

Ten county and state police departments reported to the command post at the volleyball court. The Salvation Army truck served coffee to the men.

The 'copters and the radios made it difficult to talk and hear, but the residents got the message, door to door. Their homes, they learned, were being searched.

Next to the rolled-out aerial map, someone drew careful lines through the condo layout (color-coded). "You are here." Okay, they've searched Phase I (kelly green), Cluster 5, Units 360 to 371.

Into the night bloodhounds prowled the woods. Cops with flashlights snagged their uniforms in dense thicket. And this time it wasn't just search. Closer to search and destroy. They were not looking for a kid lost in the woods. These guys kill.

Ruthie felt tired and was glad to be heading home to Nyack from work. She waited for the light to change on Route 59 before turning onto Mountainview. When she tried going up the drive to her apartment, a policeman put his hand up.

"Move it," he said.

"What do you mean, move it. I live here."

"I don't care, lady. You can't get in."

Ruthie wondered whether to argue. She decided not to; too many other cops around. Must have been an accident. Maybe something exploded. She hoped no one got hurt.

She backed away.

Ruthie headed for the A&P. Before she even had a chance to get out, she saw two state troopers jump out of their car, guns drawn, and stop a black man, who just sat in his car looking bewildered. He didn't resist at all. Ruthie saw the troopers lift up his trunk. Then they slammed it shut and motioned that he could move on. Ruthie watched him wipe his brow.

Some other neighbors, also barred from returning home, were pulling into the parking lot. Ruthie decided the best thing would be to get home and eat leftovers. She would try once more to get past the police. She turned onto Mountainview once again, past the Thruway.

"How'd I ever miss that," Ruthie said out loud, as her eye caught the wrecked car and the abandoned U-Haul. Someone was taking pictures. Must have been part of the accident, she thought. But if that's the case, why are all these cops blocking the entrance to the apartments?

Ruthie started to wonder what kind of accident had helicopters circling around so close.

"Hey lady, don't you see the roadblock?"

Ruthie noticed the officer's uniform. He's not one of ours either, she thought, but at least he isn't as brusque as the first one.

24

She decided to tell *him* she lived here; maybe he would let her through.

The officer took a look at the fiftyish, blonde-haired woman with the cross on her chest.

"Okay," he said. "Go into your apartment and shut the door."

"What happened?" she asked.

"A robbery. Two Nyack cops killed."

"What were their names, you know?"

"One of the guys was white. I don't know his name. The other was black and he had a name like Chip. Something like that, lady. Go home and turn on your TV. You'll get it all on the news."

"Chip, you're sure it's Chip?"

The cop looked impatient. Ruthie didn't bother asking again. What difference did the name make? There was only one black cop on the Nyack force and that was Chipper.

Oh, my God, she said, as she wound her way past rows of three-story brick apartments. All the terraces were empty. Ruthie felt the blood leave her head. She parked the car, rushed into her apartment, and collapsed in a chair. There was only one thing on her mind:

"Where's Mary? Does Mary know? Did anyone tell Mary that Chipper's dead?

Chipper wasn't listening. In his own way, he's as stubborn as I am, Mary thought. He just doesn't talk as much. Mary decided to give it one more try. Maybe this approach would bring him around.

"Hey, Fats, you remember that day I was waiting for a light in the brown Olds?"

Of course, Chipper remembered. How could he forget? He had never seen anyone quite like Mary. He couldn't tell if she was part-Indian, or maybe Italian. But what she was, was re-e-al offbeat. The clincher, though, was her response.

"What *are* you talking about. You're going to get me mad!" Real sassy, yet good-humored, too. But she did pull over, and he was so pleased and surprised that for a moment he gave up directing traffic. He'd tell her what he was talking about. But when he walked over and saw her behind the wheel, all he could say was, "You'll see." And give her a big smile. Later he gave her a call, and they'd been together ever since.

"Hey, Mary, how long has it been?

"Why, Fats, I knew you didn't remember. It's been ten years."

"Well, we've come a long way from that old brown car..."

"What do you mean, old brown car? That was a nice Olds. Unless you mean it's nothing compared to a brand-new Monte Carlo. Of course, we can't do any comparing if we don't have it, right?"

"Let's go pick it up now." Mary got to her pitch. "So what if you're an hour late. I'll call your job. You'll be an hour late and I'll be an hour late. We'll be late together."

Chipper wouldn't budge. "I'm not going to be late, and that's it. We'll pick it up tomorrow. What does one more day matter when we've waited this long?"

Mary didn't answer. She knew there was no arguing. He had that special twinkle that meant no more kidding. God, she knew him so well. He still looked like the big teddy bear of a man she first met.

Chipper looked at his watch ... almost two o'clock.

"C'mon, I'll drive you to work. How's that? And I'll pick you up at eleven."

Both Mary and Chipper got to work by three, on time.

Mary walked past the mirrored-glass toxicology building of Lederle Laboratories and headed for her pill-making unit.

He's really something, she thought. He does so much for

everyone else—ran around this morning, bought all those turkeys for those senior citizens out of his own pocket—and now he won't even be an hour late. He's always on the job. Of course, she also loved him because he was so dependable.

"An emergency can turn up anytime," he told her. "You remember last week when that woman went into labor right in the middle of Catherine Street, and me and Eddie delivered her. The preemie died, but at least we were there. Now just suppose I'd'a been on my way to pick up a car. Besides, you got a good job," he added. "You shouldn't be late, either."

He's right, no reason to be late. But I'm a union woman and they can't do a thing to me. I still won't take that super-vize-ory poe-sition. (She stretched the words like a wad of gum.) I'm not giving up the union for nothing.

It had been four years at Lederle. She wasted no time going there when some Federal agency leaned on them to hire blacks. The pay and the working conditions sure beat the sixteen years she put in as a nurse's aide at Nyack Hospital.

There was one thing she liked about the hospital. She met good people and they became friends. Like Ruthie, like Chipper's buddy, Eddie. She had taken care of Eddie O'Grady's father, and then a week later his mother died.

Another thing about the hospital, it gave her another bond with Chipper. Before he was a cop, Chipper worked at Rockland State Hospital as a registered nurse.

Mary had been at work barely an hour when someone said there was an important phone call.

"Mary, it's Barbara. You sitting down?"

"What's wrong?" Mary asked. She knew her best friend wouldn't be calling for nothing.

"Well, something's happened to Chipper. He's in the hospital."

"Thanks, hon. I'll call Dr. King." Mary hung up the phone.

I just knew he was running himself ragged. I told him he should have a checkup; he's been losing weight and he has high blood pressure to boot. At least he's in the hospital. They'll take good care of my Chipper there.

Mary tried phoning Nyack Hospital. She couldn't get through. That's odd; they have so many lines. Oh, well, I'll give them another try in a few minutes. She hung up the phone and sat down.

A few minutes later she was able to get through.

"Hi, this is Mary. How's my Chipper?"

"Sorry, we can't give you information over the phone."

"Well, you just better."

"Sorry."

"Then get me Dr. King, if you can't talk."

Mary waited.

"Mary, he's too busy now."

Mary decided to hang up and phone the police station. All their lines were tied up, too.

"Well, I'm not going to give up now. I'll just wait 'til they're free."

Mary lit a cigarette and waited.

The half-mile from roadblock to hospital was a stream of sirens.

At first, the hospital security guard was confused. He helped the Pearl River ambulance attendants remove the bodies from the stretchers.

"My God, it's Chip."

By the time he got to the cardiac case, his hands and wrists were covered with blood.

Minutes later a second ambulance rushed up to Emergency, this one from Nanuet. Whitmore helped carry out another stretcher; the man seemed to be a guard from Brink's. It looked like his arm was about ready to fall off.

More sirens. Another ambulance, this time from Nyack,

28

raced for the Emergency Room. But the entrance was so jammed the driver did not see another car pulling in and collided with it. The ambulance driver cursed. He had a critically wounded officer, and he wanted to get inside as soon as possible. O'Grady needed help.

Inside the hospital, Code 99 came through the loudspeakers. That was always bad news—Dead on Arrival. Then another message—Code 66. That meant action, a real emergency. They hadn't had one of those since the five kids were killed in a bus at the train crossing. And that was ten years ago. Lucky it was just a few minutes after the shift changed, the guard thought. Code 66. Once that goes out, nobody leaves.

The house surgeons raced to the Emergency Room.

"God, it's bad."

"Haven't seen so much blood since E.R. at Bellevue."

"One looks worse than the other."

Keenan was treated for his superficial stomach wound. He was released but stayed for word on Brown and O'Grady.

Another ambulance drove up.

A black man was taken out on a stretcher. Keenan recognized the man who had shot him and reached for his gun. It wasn't there. He had surrendered it when he entered the hospital.

Keenan watched the gunman being wheeled into the Emergency Room. He felt a sharp jab in his right thigh. He looked down. The bullet hadn't missed. Keenan went to look for the doctor.

A team of twelve doctors and nurses had begun to work on Chipper when the clock in the operating room said 4:16. They worked for half an hour, but there were no life signs. At 4:42 P.M. the Chief of Surgery removed his gloves. Nurses covered the body.

A nurse came out of O.R. and handed Brown's shield, bullets, and watch to the Nyack police chief.

29

"Who is it?" asked an off-duty cop.

"It's Chipper," the nurse said.

The off-duty cop walked out of the hospital. A patrol car was in front. He kicked the bumper, hard. It hurt.

Meanwhile, the chairman of the hospital's Medical Executive Committee assembled a surgical team to work on O'Grady. Once they opened him up, they found three bullet fragments in the chest and abdominal area.

As soon as they gave him one pint of blood, he seemed to lose another. They went through fourteen pints. It was not enough to stop the bleeding. After ninety minutes, the announcement came. At 6:15 P.M. O'Grady was pronounced dead.

Word on Trombino came after six hours. They saved his arm, and he was in stable condition.

At 7:15, three hours after Code 66 rang out, the hospital held a press conference.

"I've never seen anything like this here at Nyack Hospital, and I've been practicing surgery in the county for twenty-five years," said Dr. Herbert Sperling, who headed the team of surgeons.

"We are no more a nice suburban community. We are just an extension of the urban area," he told the crowd outside.

Then Dr. Sperling read off the tally. Two police officers, dead. One Brink's guard, dead. Another Brink's guard, seriously wounded. The third, with a possible concussion, in good condition. The two people injured in the collision, treated for whiplash and released. The detective slightly wounded at the roadblock when a bullet grazed his stomach, in good condition, although he was re-admitted for a newly discovered wound in his leg.

"What about the getaway driver? Is he dead?"

"John Doe, the driver, was treated for a head wound, which

was not caused by gunshot, and is now under armed guard in intensive care. Condition listed as good."

Finally, Mary got through to Dr. King. "How's my Chipper?" she asked.

"Not good, Mary."

"Is he dead?"

Dr. King paused. "Yes, Mary. Chipper's dead."

Dr. King would never lie about something like that. Still, Mary couldn't believe it. She called the police station. The word was the same.

A fellow worker came over to the phone. "Please, Mary, let me drive you home."

"Okay, but not home," Mary said. "I want to go to the station house."

The car had a hard time getting through. Broadway was lined with people, and already a crowd had assembled in front of the Village Hall.

Mary stepped out of the car.

"Chipper Brown is dead?" a young boy asked.

Mary stood for a moment staring at the boy. He trembled a bit. Behind him other youngsters all stared back.

"Yes," she answered. "Chipper Brown is dead."

As she stepped away, she could hear the word spreading. Chipper Brown's dead. They got Chipper. Mary kept her gait steady as she walked up the ramp to the Village Hall/Police Station.

"I'm Miss La Porta," Mary whispered.

"Sorry, Miss, two officers have been shot dead. There's no routine business tonight. If you have a traffic ticket, come back at a later date."

Mary stared at the officer. Then she heard a Nyack cop

whisper, "That's Chipper's girl friend." The glass door swung open and people made room.

"Sorry, Mary, he's not from Nyack."

"That's okay," she said. Then she buried her head on his shoulder and wept quietly. For some reason, she now knew it was true. Maybe it was seeing Chipper's buddies all looking so stunned. Or maybe it was the kid asking, Chipper Brown is dead?

A crowd had begun to assemble outside the Village Hall. The Village Justice stepped outside to catch a whiff of fresh air. The people seemed to be waiting for him to say something.

"It's a little smoky inside," he said.

"When are they going to be arraigned?"

"We're very close, very close," he said and went back in.

It was announced that a press conference was about to begin. Another hour elapsed. The crowd was getting restless. When eleven-thirty came and the press conference still had not started, a Baptist minister crossed over to the steps of the Village Hall. He stood at the foot of the steps and, sensing the increasing anger, addressed the crowd.

"People are hurting in there. They might need someone to pray with them tonight." That seemed to work; the crowd became quiet. A little after midnight, the press conference began. But the people did not want to be told what they already knew. They wanted to hear when the "killers" would be arraigned. "Give 'em the chair," someone yelled. The crowd surged forward, snaked its way toward the steps. Two police officers tried to restrain the crowd, but it was hard. Everyone wanted a look at the three suspects being whisked into the Village Hall. The people up front saw two women, both slight, being rushed past. One had curly dark hair; the other had deep-set eyes and high cheekbones. The most

32

noticeable thing about the man was his scraggly hair. All three were white. "Where's the driver?" someone yelled as the three suspects disappeared inside.

At last, Mary was alone. She pulled a kitchen chair into the living room and sat down.

Mary couldn't even think of the funeral arrangements. She was too angry. How could people go around killing? How could they do this? It's like I always said to him, how can people do wrong and get away with it? I sure hope they get the chair. They deserve it. Mowing down three people just for money. Of course, if Chipper hadn't been so keen on getting to work on time. But you couldn't change Fats any more than he could change me, so what's the use of thinking about that.

What gets me mad is the one who said, Please, I'm afraid of guns. I'd like to know who she is. Someone at the station house said it was the same one they caught on the road, screaming: I didn't do it, they did it. Figures. That type, who warns the guys inside that there's guns so they could open up and start blasting away without warning, that's the same type to run for her life and blame the others. A real rat.

I have to find out who she is. They said her name is Barbara Edson, but you never know if people like that are telling the truth. If they knew when the Brink's truck was making its pickup and were all prepared with getaway cars and what not, they probably figured out some aliases, too. You don't give your real name when you have guns. Not if you plan to use them. Of that, Mary was certain.

If he'd just been an hour late... the thought crept up on her every now and then, and Mary didn't like it. She wanted to find out what was going on. No "what if this" and "what if that." She wanted to know, who is this Barbara Edson? If she hadn't opened her mouth in that truck and alerted the guys in the back, Chip would still be alive....

Mary watched it get dark. Today was the day we were going to pick up the Monte Carlo. She shuddered, annoyed at the thought, and turned on the news. Maybe they know more about her now. Edson's the one I'd like to get first. I'd kill her if she came here. "I'm afraid of guns." That's a good one. Mary didn't laugh.

Chipper's face shared the screen with O'Grady's. Then a new face.

The newscaster said Barbara Edson's real name was Katherine Boudin. And she wasn't a bank robber. She was famous. A revolutionary. Weather Underground. She was in a Greenwich Village town house that exploded. A bomb factory. She escaped, but three of her friends were killed. After that, she went underground.

Mary went straight to the phone. She knew someone who lived in the Village.

"I'm okay. Listen. Who's this Katherine Boudin?"

The friend repeated the information about the town-house explosion. Mary cut her off. She already knew that.

What she didn't know was about the family, that Kathy Boudin's father was a well-known civil rights attorney.

"Well, this is what I want to know. If her father is this famous lawyer, is he going to help her get prosecuted now?" Mary asked.

"Of course not. He says he's going to do everything to get her the best legal help available."

Mary felt a sudden rage. "I thought you said this Leonard Boodeen is a famous civil rights lawyer. Didn't you say that?"

"But Mary, this is his own child. Don't you understand?"

"I understand just fine. But you know, Chipper was someone's child, too."

"Mary, Mary, are you okay?"

Mary couldn't answer. For some reason the thought of

34

Waverly being someone's child, Fats, who was so nurturing to her, made him seem extra vulnerable. But as soon as she thought of this Boudin girl being defended by her father, Mary composed herself.

"I've got to check out this Mr. Boodeen for myself."

Leonard Boudin stood for a moment, adjusting the collar of his mackintosh. He was not accustomed to having a protective phalanx accompany him to court. A photographer jumped over the barricades and started snapping.

Mary did not like Boudin on sight. He looked vain to her, standing there, talking to the press, like he was a star. Mary did not know which made her more angry, the father being treated like a star, or the daughter. Where was the mother? She hadn't seen too much about her. Only one thing pleased Mary: he couldn't enter Nyack without police protection. They might treat him like a movie star in the city, but up here he was like the Mafia.

It had been a confusing week. Chipper died Tuesday. What was today? Friday. It seemed so long ago and at the same time as if it just happened. That was what it must mean to lose touch with reality.

On TV, she saw police officers surround the Village Hall. The building, in fact the whole village, looked under siege. There on the screen, she saw the river right down at the bottom of the steep hill alongside the Village Hall, but it was hard to recognize Nyack. She saw the Village Hall all draped in purple and black bunting and the two large bouquets of flowers flanking the ramp. The combination of flowers and guns seemed so weird.

She knew that the sight of the suspects would make it all real again. Even seeing this famous lawyer on TV was enough to make it all real. Mary was sure she heard him tell a reporter his daughter was innocent. That must mean he thinks she didn't do anything wrong. How could he, she asked herself, working up an anger.

"Good thing he does have protection," she joked with Barbara, "or I'd be after him."

"Why him? Why not the daughter?" her best friend asked.

"Both of them. You bet. I'd get both of them. One lies while the other swears it's true."

"Here she comes. There. A police car just drove up."

Mary watched the four suspects—all shackled—being rushed in, past a small group saluting, with clenched fists, the "October 20 Freedom Fighters."

"Freedom Fighters," Mary snorted. "It's lucky they're wearing bullet-proof vests is all I have to say."

"C'mon, Mary, everyone knows you wouldn't hurt a fly. You're all talk."

"Not this time."

In the packed courtroom, Leonard Boudin put his arms around his daughter and kissed her with great passion.

Kathy was dressed in brown prison pants, white slippers, a green shirt, and blue sweat jacket. But even more startling than the red letters, R.C. Jail, on the jacket were her deep-set blue eyes and the high cheekbones.

Clark sat down. She had two black eyes. Gilbert sat down. His cheeks were visibly bruised.

Brown looked in bad shape. He had on a neck brace and he was moaning.

"Act like a man," a guard told him.

Brown leaned back. Another guard pushed him forward. Attorney Susan Tipograph yelled, "You're torturing him. This man is in pain."

"Oh, really. What a pity," commented a guard near a back

36

door. Standing next to him was a large New York State Police dog.

When the judge was seated, the defense attorneys went to work. They advised the four—all charged with three counts of second-degree murder and all held without bail—not to give their names.

"They should not be in jail. They have already had to endure severe brutality. And there is no evidence to keep them," one argued.

The Rockland District Attorney, Kenneth Gribetz, rose. He held up the death certificates of Officers Brown and O'Grady. "This, I submit, is evidence of murder." Leonard Boudin, his arm around his daughter, drew her close to him. Kathy was staring absently.

It was almost three o'clock. Brown was wailing loudly. The defense attorneys requested a short recess.

The guards stood up next to Brown. His hands were shackled to thick steel chains padlocked around his waist. They buoyed him up so he could get to a bathroom. Brown was barefoot but for a torn part of a black sneaker. He looked like a slave being sold at auction.

A few minutes later he was escorted back, his green prison pants resting around his ankles, his bare buttocks exposed. Kathy Boudin and Tipograph bent over and helped him lift his pants.

It was getting close to six o'clock. A decision was announced to the reporters. Village Justice Robert P. Lewis denied a motion to drop the charges and free the four.

The reporters rushed to phones, practically stampeding the heavily armed guards leading the four suspects out of court.

Tipograph gently pressed Kathy Boudin's arm. "See you tomorrow," she whispered.

"I hope so," a guard said sarcastically.

"I hope everyone heard that," the attorney yelled out. "He said, 'I hope so.'" Then she and the other defense attorneys put the court papers into their attaché cases. Reporters, lights flashing behind, ran up to them, but the attorneys were not talking. They walked down the wooden stairs and out the building past the guards bearing shotguns and automatic pistols, who were still standing, in the rain, on the rooftops and all around the Village Hall.

Hours later at the Village Hall, a crowd of a different mood assembled. It was somber. Little talk. Mary handed Barbara a white candle and took one for herself. Then she joined the others walking south on Broadway.

In the rain, the village shops seemed to merge. The black crepe streamed across The Crafters, The Hand of the Craftsman, Liberty Crafts, The Thieves' Market, Blue Willow, Priscilla Antiques, Timeless Treasures—all the shops with their art nouveau glass and their art deco frames, the primitives and the Orientalia, Wedgwood, cut glass, wicker, pine chests, pressed glass, frames, and prints—"Nyack Cares" was the message.

The whole village seemed to be walking in the rain. A dream of a town for hippies, for craftsfolk, for elegant antique collectors, for ethnic boutique owners, who did not disturb the old three-story buildings when they put in their sunbursts and air conditioners.

In the distance glowed the long sweep of the Tappan Zee Bridge. The lights of the bridge on a clear night looked like just another collectible antique necklace. Tonight the rain muted everything and blurred the memory of Nyack as a town that spoke of both prosperity and something funky, long after the Nyack Indians gathered to pick oysters at the river's edge. A town that New Yorkers fled to when cholera broke out in the city and were pleased to find so compatible, so gracious, a mere thirty miles away.

Nyack never closed itself off. How could it? Nyack was, and is, a river village. The lighthouse at the dock may house boutiques, but the place retains a flavor of the pirate, the vagabond, the alien.

For amidst Victorian splendor dwells one of the largest Haitian communities in the nation.

As she walked, Mary could hear the patois of men who worked in the auto repair shop behind Liberty Crafts. She recognized their brightly colored knit caps.

The crowd stopped at the corner of DePew and Broadway in front of a many-gabled house of cranberry red with large signs in the window: Ambulette Service—Oxygen. Diagonally across was the Hugh E. White Funeral Home. Mary gazed at the gracious, white, colonnaded house with its chocolate shutters. How right that Chipper is resting inside. It's so southern; it's as if he's come back home to Virginia.

The honor guard in white gloves and black-ribboned shields smiled at Mary; she could see several had been crying. Mary walked up to the steel casket. She looked down at Waverly. The guards turned their heads. Mary knelt by the coffin. He looks as if he has a joke he's going to tell.

"Fats," she whispered, "you're too much."

Then she stood up and went over to kiss Waverly's mother and his two daughters, who had flown in for the funeral. Waverly's mother embraced Mary as if she were a child of her own. And then Mary asked one of Chipper's buddies to lead her to O'Grady's wife.

After the funeral, Mary did not follow Waverly to Oak Hill Cemetery. She made her way to her own church. There was another funeral to endure.

At 11:45, down a street barely a block from the Pilgrim Baptist Church, the bells of St. Ann's Roman Catholic

Church tolled every ten seconds. Then at noon, they stopped. In an eerie repeat of the morning's service, the funeral for Sergeant O'Grady began. Again, the sound of drums, the salutes, the flag-draped casket, the pallbearers in uniform, and the bagpipe's "Amazing Grace." A few details had changed.

Where Pilgrim Baptist often rang to electric guitar and gospel, a somber organ sounded as St. Ann's service began. With its tree-shaded English Gothic façade and the carved woodwork in its gables, St. Ann's and its rectory evoked an Ivy League serenity.

Pilgrim Baptist—on a bare street, the green hills rising beyond—stood across from Ernestine's Beauty Spot and a Doberman in a chain-link fenced yard. To the left, across High Avenue, was a parking lot and a white low-slung factory where Haitian women assembled each morning.

Pilgrim had bare, white, stucco walls within, brown rafters and eaved roof above. Here, at St. Ann's, parishioners moved along a wide aisle under hand-carved arches. River breezes rotated the fans mounted above the aisle. The walls depicted in relief the last days of Jesus.

Pilgrim Baptist worshipers entered and left past a movable bulletin board with thumbtacked posters. Food stamps make a difference. Gospel Heavyweights in a battle of songs. And the dominant stained-glass front window with the legend: In memory of all departed members/by the members 1877-1974.

St. Ann's parishioners moved past leaflets tucked in wooden pockets. Natural family planning. Tuition tax credits. Books: *Staying Faithful.* And a plaque: The National Association of Pastoral Musicians/Outstanding Parish Award 1981/Outstanding Achievement in Musical Liturgy at the Parish Level.

Mary La Porta, once a Harlem babe, was a parishioner of St. Ann's.

At this funeral, O'Grady's wife, Diane, thirty-three, now his widow, took the folded flag. Ed, also thirty-three, had been younger than Waverly, who was forty-five. The priest did not speak of an unjust God. He did not seem inclined to ask, Why Chipper? Why O'Grady? Instead he spoke of the sorrow a mother feels when a child goes off to school for the first time. "Yet she rejoices," he reminded the mourners as he spoke of the earth as a beginning, an entrance, the entrance to Eternity.

O'Grady's coffin was closed and draped with a gold flag, the flag of the Church. The fire engine was waiting.

Late that afternoon, close to dusk, Mary was back home. She stepped outside her apartment. It was a clear night; she could feel the chill mountain air mingle with the breeze off the water. At least it's quiet again. Mary stepped back inside. Chipper's family had insisted she take one entire floral arrangement, but she didn't like how it looked in the apartment; it reminded her of the funeral parlor. She took out several carnations and lilies and walked down Mountainview to the intersection. There, at the entrance to the Thruway, she knelt by the two wreaths and candle that marked the spot. She did not know which was for Chipper and which for Ed, but what did it matter?

Mary remembered the time Chipper was called to the home of a black woman in the midst of a domestic argument. The woman stared at Chipper's partner. "I didn't ask for no white cop," she shouted.

"Then you didn't ask for any cop," Chipper told her before they left.

41

Mary placed the flowers between the wreaths and made her way back up the hill.

Suddenly she felt a surge of anger. Kathy Boudin, handcuffed, flashed in front of her. The image was so clear, it was just like watching TV all over again. She appeared to be smiling. Mary couldn't believe it.

Then Mary remembered her best friend's words, "Don't worry, hon, she won't be smiling for long; she's going straight back to jail."

# 2

# KATHY'S PRISON OBSERVATIONS

UNITED STATES DISTRICT COURT
SOUTHERN DISTRICT OF NEW YORK
----------------------------------------------------x
KATHIE BOUDIN, et ano.,

                    Petitioners    81 Civ. 7190 (KTD)

      —against—           AFFIDAVIT

_____ ,* ET AL.,

               Respondents.
----------------------------------------------------x
STATE OF NEW YORK   )
                      : SS.:
COUNTY OF NEW YORK )

KATHIE BOUDIN, being duly sworn, deposes and says:

1. This statement is my description of the conditions I have been forced to live under during the past 7 weeks at the Metropolitan Correctional Center in New York.

**A. ISOLATION**

2. I live in solitary confinement. The prison word is "administrative detention" but that does not describe it. When I am

---

*The names of prison personnel have been deleted from the affidavit.

43

awakened at 6:30 A.M. I wake up in a room 12′ x 8′ where I will spend the next 18 hours alone until I go to bed again. I see my mother two times a week, attorneys, and have brief exchanges with guards. Otherwise I am alone in a tiny room. I have not been allowed to talk with my codefendant about the preparation for the trial, about our children, about anything. I am not allowed to talk with other prisoners with whom I could share the experience of being in prison, gain and give support, and simply have normal human relationships. I cannot have friends visit me from outside prison. I have been totally isolated from any community of friends inside the prison walls or outside.

3. The prison is cutting me off from a necessary part of any and every human being's life. The need for talking to people, building friendships, sharing day-to-day life. Solitary confinement is understood to be a process designed to break people down emotionally and mentally. Solitary confinement is a very lonely experience.

4. This isolation from human beings is designed as a form of torture to break me down because of my political beliefs and history. As is evident from prison records, the severity of the charge against me is not the basis of the solitary confinement policy. Other prisoners with similar charges have not been kept in solitary confinement for such a long time, with no end in sight. This is done to me solely because of my politics. Under the guise of "security," it is designed to destroy me as a human being, as a political woman, and to make it difficult for me, mentally or physically, to prepare for or stand trial.

5. At 6:30 A.M. each morning I hear a bang on my door, and breakfast is brought in. Many times the tray is placed on my open toilet seat. My room is 12′ by 8′ with only a bed, an open toilet, and a sink in it.

6. For the first four weeks the entire lighting in my cell consisted of one 60-watt bulb over the sink and toilet at one end of the room. In order to get enough light to read I had to sit

on the open toilet or move my bed next to the open toilet to catch the light. After a month my eyesight had severely deteriorated. Finally the prison put in a glaring 135-watt high-intensity bulb with no shade. The only window has bars on it and looks only into walls. There is a sense of day or night, but nothing in between—no sun, no ability to see the sky, no sense of the weather, just gray light or darkness. Only when I go to an attorney visit, make a phone call or take my hour recreation do I catch a glimpse of the sky. Only in the afternoon is there a sense of the sun.

7. The window is hermetically sealed. I have not had any fresh air since October 26, 1981, almost two months ago, when I arrived at MCC [Metropolitan Correction Center]. I am not allowed to exercise on the roof with the other women.

8. I live in essentially a box cut off from the rest of the world—no sense of time of day, no sense of weather, no fresh air, no people. If I do not want to spend 22½ hours sitting or sleeping and eating on my bed, I can walk in my room. The space allows me to walk six steps and turn around and walk six steps back to the back wall. After doing this for a few minutes, I get somewhat dizzy. These conditions are designed to break me not only mentally but also physically.

9. Over a two-week period in late November the temperature in my room ranged from 85° - 95°. I had to take off my clothes in the presence of male guards and to live in front of them in a bra and underpants, using a wet towel to keep water on my body. At night I had to sleep nude on the floor to try to get below the heat. Even the sheet was too warm. There was no air. Whenever I complained I was told the heating system was faulty so that when it is hot where I am it is cold elsewhere in the prison. Supposedly nothing could be done. The heat might not have been so bad if the space were not 8′ × 12′ with no fresh air.

10. My door has a narrow window on it covered by steel mesh. When I wish to talk to a guard I have to yell through the

door and look through wire mesh. Now, with the glaring unshielded 135-watt bulb by the door I have trouble seeing out the door.

11. My only so-called "recreation" takes place in the small hallway right outside my room and the other segregation rooms. It is only three small steps by eighteen small steps. A big desk with two male guards sits in the middle of the floor. Lieutenants and other prison personnel constantly sit there to fill out various logbooks and forms relating to us. It is ludicrous to call this "recreation." I lie down to exercise on a dirty floor and move out of the way as lieutenants and guards walk by me. I have to make sure my clothes do not pull up on me, as the two male guards sitting at the desk watch me exercise.

12. I am not allowed to talk to any other prisoners. They prohibit me even from talking through the doors to my codefendant. This is transparently punitive since to speak through the door requires yelling, so that the guards would hear out every word.

13. Throughout the day various categories of prison officials come trooping up to our doors. Each one bangs loudly on the door. Often instead of opening it to have a face-to-face discussion, they yell through the door as I place my face against steel mesh to try to see and hear them, as if to remind me that I am in a cage cut off from all human relationships.

14. In a typical encounter a few days ago, Lt. — opened my door and said, "Is everything all right?" I said, "No, this 135-watt bulb is blinding, can I get a lamp?" He said, "That's not my area, ask Mr. —." I said, "What *is* your area? What should I raise with you?" He said, "Don't worry about it," and slammed the door, then logged in the record that he had seen me.

15. Many nights I am awakened by guards kicking or banging on the door. They say they do it to make us move to make sure we are here. At times I hear them laughing after they kick the door.

16. It has been said by the prison I get out each day, sometimes for several hours, to attorney visits. Even a few hours out of a day when there are sixteen waking hours totally alone, and no right to speak to any human being but a guard, does not break the dehumanizing solitude. Moreover, my lawyers have legal work to do; they cannot spend all their time providing personal contact and support for me. Moreover, my relationship to an attorney is no substitute for relationships with other women here to help deal with the difficulty of the prison experience. It is no substitute for having the ability to talk as much as possible to my codefendant(s) about the trial preparation and strategy. And my legal visits are not a substitute for being able to have a connection to my own friends and the community outside prison.

17. I was placed in solitary confinement only because I was classified "high security." No evidence was presented to me. I had no ability to challenge whatever information this decision supposedly was based on. For almost two months, until this court proceeding, I have been living under inhuman conditions with no ability to challenge the classification which put me here. I have been told that no behavior of mine at the institution can change this classification. No matter how well I behave, I must remain in this box.

The notion that MCC plans to keep me in solitary confinement month after month, that there is no behavior of mine that could affect this classification, can only be designed to present to me a very bleak and inhuman future, to try to destroy me as a political person, as a woman with a heart and soul, to break me physically, and to make me a defendant at trial unprepared and unable to defend myself.

## B. SEPARATION FROM MY CHILD

18. The MCC forbids me from touching my fifteen-month-old baby, Chesa. Judith Clark cannot touch her twelve-month-

47

old baby either. We are told we cannot touch them because of security. It is said they might be carrying a weapon in their Pampers. Yet although we object to it, we are willing to have our babies searched and their Pampers changed before the visit in order to be able to hold them. But since the prison administration had decided to punish us, it refuses to reconsider its policy.

19. We finally decided to see our children even knowing we could not touch them. At the start of the visit Mr. —, said, "If you touch your child even once, the visit will be immediately discontinued." Then, carrying out orders of the warden, he proceeded for two hours to watch every move of the babies through a glass window. Every time my child would nearly place his hand on my knee, I would jump away for fear the visit would be discontinued. Judith Clark's child came toward her with arms outstretched and Judith Clark had to back away, while the grandparents tried to divert the child and the baby cried because her mother was backing away from her instead of reaching out to her outstretched arms. It was so horrible that Judith Clark's parents had to take the baby away early.

20. My love for my baby was always communicated through hugging, kissing, holding. My child of course does not talk yet, so touch is the most important way to communicate. This is true for all babies and mothers. I could not express my love for my child and he, of course, felt that and he could not touch me. He could not feel my body. He could not smell me. I cannot express in words the pain that such cruelty inflicts on both me and my child.

## C. MEDICAL ABUSE

21. There are many examples of punitive medical treatment. I feel I must also tell how some of my codefendants are being treated. When Lt. — was on duty, Judith Clark's and Eve

48

Rosahn's toilets overflowed, flooding their floors and the hallway outside. Judith Clark and Eve Rosahn picked everything off from their floor. Judith Clark had just gotten back from Rockland County where she had had an abortion a few hours before. She was bleeding and pale. A guard had women inmates come clean the hallway and allowed Judith Clark and Eve Rosahn out into the hallway until plumbers could come and repair the toilets. Their rooms were not only filled with three inches of water on the floor but smelled of sewage. When Lt. — arrived he immediately sent Clark and Rosahn back in their rooms where they sat on their bed for another two and a half hours in a room flooded with sewage, Judith Clark just having gotten back from an operation and bleeding. There was nothing "dangerous" about allowing them out of their rooms until they could be cleaned. There are empty rooms across the hall where they could have waited. But Lt. — insisted they sit on their beds in a room flooded with sewage, a situation dangerous for Judith Clark in terms of infection and unhealthy for anyone.

22. There is no need to repeat the chronology of the prison obstructing my ability to get eyeglasses. For weeks I sat in my cell unable even to read. When I left for "recreation," I could not even move quickly because I could not see. This was totally unnecessary. Each obstruction was justified by "security." The guards insist I do not really need glasses and imply I was making a fuss about nothing.

23. As a result of almost six weeks without glasses my eyes are strained and I am still in pain. I cannot evaluate whether my glasses are correct, whether the eyes need treatment, whether time will repair them. However, I have requested to see an opthamologist—an eye doctor of the prison's choosing—in order to evaluate my eyes. The prison authorities have refused. I have, in the alternative, offered to have an opthamologist, acceptable to the prison, whom I will pay, come in to

see me whenever the prison wants. They still refuse. So far, since arriving at MCC I have seen a woman who can only prescribe glasses. The first visit with her led to an incorrect prescription. The second visit with her—resulting from my attorneys' argument in court—led to an improved prescription but it is not clear it is correct. I was sent a psychiatrist and an internist when I asked to see an eye doctor. Neither of them can perform refractions or evaluate my eye condition.

24. When I had my second optometrist examination I asked for a copy of the prescription. Mr. — said he had been told not to give me a copy of the prescription. I said I have a right to a copy of the prescription of my own eyes. It was clear he had no authority to countermand.

25. Moreover, the optometrist had neglected to write in the book the first prescription she had given me and she now had changed the prescription. I wanted a copy of the new prescription to give to my family optometrist so they could compare the difference between the first and second prescription. But Mr. — refused to give it to me. I filled out a protest, my attorneys wrote two letters, and I finally was given a copy of the prescription.

26. The clinic where Judith Clark had her abortion told her to absolutely have a two week checkup, so the MCC's GYN department scheduled it for her. She was at an attorney visit on the third floor when the GYN office located on the second floor called her for her appointment. They could have called her in the attorney room (that has happened with me) and the guard watching her in the attorney room (we are escorted everywhere so there is always a guard with us) could have taken her to the GYN. Instead Lt. — who was outside our rooms when the doctor call came, told the guard, "Just tell them to reschedule the appointment, for next week, or next month, or maybe next year." This answer typifies the sarcastic, sadistic approach of Lt. — towards us; moreover, he had no reason

50

to not call the third floor and give Judy the chance to go to her appointment on the day when the clinic had said she should definitely have an appointment. She had to wait another week.

### D. INTERFERENCE WITH THE PREPARATION OF OUR DEFENSE

27. Only as of this week can I meet with codefendant and counsel in the MCC and sometimes those joint meetings are still denied. We have not yet been able to meet with our three other codefendants to discuss the complicated issues of the trial. Judith Clark and I are prohibited by Mr. — from holding legal conferences with each other except in the presence of an attorney. Even the Court appearances in Rockland are scheduled on separate days so that we cannot have joint counsel visits.

28. In the attorney room we are obligated to sit in the open room rather than the enclosed rooms. We sit by a large window where a guard watches us from only a few feet away. Other prisoners waiting for attorneys wander around us, to the water fountain, pacing up and down. This leads to a situation where the attorney-client privacy is constantly violated. Guards and other people can read writing, overhear conversations, etc. There are times when attorneys have had to wait up to an hour to see us because they cannot find someone to escort us.

### E. ARBITRARY RESTRICTIONS

29. Mr. — and the Lieutenants also impose punitive methods by arbitrarily changing conditions at whim or by harassing us with unnecessary restrictions. For example, on December 17, 1981, I tried to reach my attorneys, Martin Garbus and Victor Rabinowitz, to discuss the proceedings before this Court. I made two phone calls, but neither attorney was at his home or office. I was on the phone five or six minutes trying to locate them. At around 8:30 A.M. I told the

guard since I had been unable to reach my attorney, I wanted to try later. The guard said, "That's your phone call for the day." When I objected, Lt. — confirmed that that was my phone call for the day. When Lt. — came, I told him I wished another chance to call. The other guard on duty said he had no problem walking the ten steps to the phone with me at some point in the day. Lt. — said, "I understand you were on the phone awhile." I turned to Guard —, who had escorted me to the phone (which, as I say, is about a fifteen second walk from my room), and he said, "You weren't on the phone that long. Just as soon as I saw you make contact I marked down that was your phone call for the day." I said, "But Mr. Garbus' wife answered and said he wasn't there." Lt. — said, "But you might be lying." As a result I was not allowed to make any other phone call that day. Sometimes when we make a phone call and we cannot reach the desired person, there is no problem in trying again. Then one day or for several days suddenly the rules change as they did in the example above. Other prisoners can call all day as many numbers as they want.

30. I must make a written request for every single thing. The officials would not let us get watches from our family so that we could develop a sense of time. It took us from November 25, 1981, when the first request was made for a watch until December 18, 1981, to acquire watches, in spite of many written and oral requests. My mother dropped off a Timex watch which they said they could not accept because of security even though Timex was the correct kind. Then they could not figure out how to deal with buying the watches. This went on for weeks.

31. When we first arrived we were able to take our phone call, so-called "recreation" and showers between 8:30 A.M. and 8:30 P.M. During that time there are two guards sitting outside our door, able to escort us to attorney visits, phone calls, etc. Suddenly one day the rule was changed so that we were not

allowed out of our room after 4:00 P.M. for anything except attorney visits. Last week a new memo came signed by —, announcing a new policy that we had to take our hour "recreation" at 8:00 A.M. or it would be written down as a refusal.

Since 8:00 A.M. is just when we have awakened and have 16 lonely isolated hours ahead of us, it is healthier for the mind and body for us to try to get out of the box in the middle of the day.

32. The guards assigned to us do nothing but sit there watching us and writing in books when we take our showers, recreation, attorney visits, etc. The policy of forcing us to take recreation at 8:00 A.M. or 9:00 A.M. is designed to punish us further, isolate us further. There may be a day when it is urgent to reach someone at night, about a legal or personal matter; now we cannot make any calls after 4:00 P.M.

33. Another policy designed to harass us, and to eliminate simple means of surviving the hardship of solitary confinement, concerns plastic crochet needles. I requested plastic crochet needles to help pass time. Every other female inmate can get them. The warden's policy was no plastic crochet needles because they are dangerous. However we get plastic ballpoint pens with a hooked cover from the commissary. We have a radio from the commissary with a long metal antenna. It is punitive to deny us plastic crochet needles to help ease the boredom.

34. When our rooms were extremely overheated Mr. — let us have a thermometer to keep a record of the temperature in the hottest rooms. Each time a guard would see the thermometer they would come in and snatch it out of the room accusingly, saying, "You can't have that." Even when I said, "Mr. — said I could," they would keep it, making it impossible to keep the temperature record.

35. Since we do not know what the other prisoners eat we do not know if we get the same food they do. We did learn,

however, that each prisoner gets salad. This was missing from our trays for the first week. I finally insisted on it and now get it.

36. The Guards stop our mail and take our personal belongings. I was being strip-searched one day in the guards' supply closet and noticed a stack of six or seven paperbacks. They were for Eve Rosahn. It turned out some guard had just put the books in the closet instead of giving them to her.

37. I was called to an attorney visit. The guard on duty made me take off my clothes before leaving my room. Normal procedure is to make us take off our clothes after the attorney visit. On the way to the elevator one of the other inmates said "hi" to me while I was waiting for the elevator. Some time later, I tugged at my underpants since I had my period and was straightening my Kotex. Guard — immediately yelled go back inside, and yelled to —, "She had contact with other prisoners, strip-search her." I was taken back to my room and strip-searched completely for a second time by two women guards. The other woman prisoner had said all of one word, "hi," and hadn't been near enough to touch me. — escalated the situation into a security crisis.

38. Each day some new regulation is changed. One day Mr. — said we can only get hot water from the coffee urn in the kitchen when we are out of our showers. Otherwise we have to get it from the tap in our sink. Normally with our meals and sometimes at night the guard will take the 30-second walk to the kitchen and bring us a cup of water. But that day because — suddenly had this new rule, we couldn't get the boiled water to make tea. Again, for one day, there was a new rule and then it was back to normal.

39. These are only a few examples of which there are hundreds. It is a difficult situation. All of these forms of harassment and punishment take their toll and it is necessary to protest them in order to survive. On the other hand, I

sometimes find so much time and involvement taken up by filling out one form or another in protest that my entire life becomes one of protesting these harassments. It is very draining. Part of the purpose of the punishment and harassments is to wear us down.

_____

KATHIE BOUDIN

Sworn to before me
this ___ day of December, 1981

_____

Notary Public

Kathy's isolation was soon ended. Federal Judge Kevin T. Duffy agreed the conditions of her imprisonment were inhumane and ordered an end to her solitary confinement at the Metropolitan Correction Center. Shortly after Duffy's decision, Kathy was transferred to state custody at Woodbourne Correction Center.

# PART TWO

# *REACTION*

# 3

# KATHY BEFORE BRINK'S

"'LET me show you a picture of a wonderful girl,' Leonard Boudin said to a friend; whereupon, he pulled from his wallet a picture of his young daughter, Kathy. It was a composite of mug shots taken by the Chicago police department. The same pictures that are on the FBI's poster; Hoover placed her on the Most Wanted List shortly after her father became involved in the Harrisburg defense," writes a journalist who covered the trial.

I know the Boudins and so it's easy for me to visualize this scene. Leonard taking out the picture, neither boastful nor self-pitying but with a touch of grace and a smile that communicated a wistful ambivalence—the pride he felt for his daughter's uncompromising stance and the occasional twinge of fear for its consequences. Kathy had always followed whatever route she felt she had to; it was as if his daughter possessed a freedom Leonard could only wish for. She was the true rebel, and he, a mere defender of the rebel.

Of course, there might come a time when Kathy would get caught up in something he couldn't handle. But it was hard to imagine his dark, intense daughter, with her passionate, striking looks, doing anything from which he couldn't, ultimately, bail her out.

As far back as Leonard could remember, Kathy had been

stubborn, but she had also been right. Even when Elizabeth Irwin High School—the private school chosen for its liberal reputation—asked Kathy to quit team sports because she was better than the boys, she balked. Many would have agreed that tennis was a more suitable game than baseball or basketball, but not Leonard, I imagine. Yes, basketball's a boy's sport, but it's street boys, often blacks. And besides, it's not a sport natural to someone short. And Kathy, like her father, is short. And like him, she enjoyed a challenge. For basketball is a game of feints, angles, and strategies.

When the time came for college, Kathy did not pick Antioch, Bard, Swarthmore, or any other of the progressive schools. Instead, she chose Bryn Mawr where freshmen were advised to bring along a tea service. The Gothic campus with its towers, arches, and lawns, and its close location to the old money of Main Line Philadelphia was quite a contrast to Leonard's humble alma maters—City College and St. John's Law School in Brooklyn. But Bryn Mawr was not all etiquette and impeccable social standing. It had a strong academic program and a long Quaker heritage that must have been appealing to Jean, Kathy's mother, who is a pacifist.

By the time Kathy had finished her freshman year, she had helped put out a peace supplement to the school paper, had set up a disarmament group, and had been elected president of the Alliance for Political Affairs—a record to make any liberal parent proud.

By sophomore year, Kathy was already on the move, organizing an enormous conference on civil rights that amounted to the first campus teach-in. When she encountered a liberal professor who hadn't shown up, she asked him point blank where he was. And when he told her he went to a party, Kathy became furious. "Well, for chrissakes, how dare you teach that stuff in class and then when it comes time to actually do something, you're out partying."

Picking up the mixed signals of the liberal professors, Kathy began to shift her focus away from the academy. With the same energy that enabled her to steal a base or land a jump shot, she organized the black janitors and maids on campus and started the first all-woman alternative style co-op dormitory. This shift, though subtle at the time, was an early introduction, a leitmotiv, of Kathy's later involvement with blacks on the one hand and women on the other.

By now it was clear that Kathy could get things done. In November of '63, Kathy and three other students picketed an overcrowded black school. Picketing, of course, was nothing new. She had already done that in high school. But this time she took it one step further and, again, a leitmotiv played in the background as Kathy wound up in jail. The school was shocked and even talked about disciplinary action.

Kathy was not intimidated in the least and sent off a letter to the school paper. "It is alleged that being arrested is a violation of the self-governing rules, that it brings discredit upon the college. This implies that being arrested is in itself discreditable and is based on the assumption that law is an end in itself. I believe that law is a means to an end as are methods of negotiation such as meetings and letters. If desired ends cannot be achieved within the law or by normally accepted methods of negotiation, then new methods must be adopted," Kathy wrote. The letter was printed on November 22, 1963, the day President John Kennedy was assassinated. With the blood from John Kennedy's brains still fresh on Jackie's suit, it must have seemed quite absurd to be worrying about the proper way to express concern, as if injustice were akin to serving tea. Kathy's arrest changed activism from a disgrace to a source of school pride.

Only Jean saw things differently. Although far too sophisticated to worry about disgracing venerable old Bryn Mawr or to consider going to jail for social protest dishonorable, she

61

nevertheless was worried. Kathy was opting for high adventure, and high adventure didn't get you into medical school. If Kathy was serious about becoming a doctor, she had better settle down to academic study.

Leonard bailed Kathy out, and Kathy continued her course.

By her senior year, Kathy had had it with the academic environment. For three years she had studied Russian language and literature; now she wanted to live in Russia. Although college policy mandated that students spend their last year on campus, Kathy, with the help of Rockwell Kent, her father's client, had no trouble convincing the school to change its policy. (Leonard had successfully fought for Kent's right to visit Russia, and Kent now intervened on Kathy's behalf for the same "right.")

For most of us, living alone in Russia in 1964 might have been an awesome challenge. But Kathy thrived on challenge; also she was, by now, an experienced traveler. At 16 she had gone to France to improve her language skills. And in 1961, during her freshman year at Bryn Mawr, when Kathy's father was in Cuba representing Castro's new government, Kathy traveled to Cuba. But instead of staying with Leonard, she stayed with some Cuban students.

"I remember on January 2, 1961—I was seventeen years old—standing in downtown Havana, surrounded by a million people, a million Cubans who had come to Havana to celebrate the Revolution. At the end of the six or seven hours of people celebrating, came a long military parade with guns, and weapons, and tanks. I had been cheering along with everybody else when I suddenly realized that I was cheering for tanks and guns, which was something that was completely opposite to what I had been brought up to do."

Kathy's Cuban friend, noticing the tears in her eyes, confessed that he, too, disliked weapons but felt the United States forced his country to arm itself, according to the movie *Underground,* made by Emile de Antonio, Mary Lampson, and Haskell Wexler in 1975.

Kathy was learning that if she was to become a real revolutionary, she couldn't use her feelings as a guide. Quickly, she corrected herself, lining up her feelings with her head instead of her heart. Revolution required a tougher stance than the pacifist one her mother had taught her.

When Kathy returned home from Russia for graduation, she graduated magna cum laude, despite Jean's concerns. Yet she did not return to the academy or to medical school. Drawn again to blacks and women, she took off for Cleveland to work with black welfare mothers. It was they who gave the sense of hope for the future, missing in Russia and at Bryn Mawr.

In *Underground* she describes riding through downtown Hough, the place of the Cleveland riots. It was the day after the riots, and she was with a black welfare mother and her two children. Although the street was lined with tanks, soldiers and guns, they turned the radio up loud and drove along singing, as if the weapons didn't exist. The welfare mother told Kathy she had every intention of getting what was coming to her, guns or no guns.

When Jean visited Kathy in Cleveland, she was appalled. Roaches and rats were a far cry from medical school. If Kathy wanted to help the poor, why didn't she become a doctor? That way, she could raise the standards of everyone, instead of lowering them for herself. Or as Jean put it, "Her big accomplishment was learning how to live on sixty cents a day."

Yet, I can imagine Jean being put down for her response, the liberal men calling it "bourgeois," not understanding that what Jean wanted for her daughter was what it seems she could not have for herself—an independent life with work that had both meaning and respect.

But there was no way that Jean, a woman dependent on her husband for support, could compete with the gutsy black welfare mothers. Kathy stayed on in Cleveland for four years, the amount of time it would have taken to complete medical school.

It was now 1968—a big year for student radicals. To help heat things up, our country launched the Vietcong Tet Offensive in January and February. By April, campuses all over were in revolt. Students ripped off the cloak of respectability that school administrators had hidden under and exposed them for what they were: collaborators in the war, and sneaky ones at that, with their classified research and secret Defense Department contracts.

God, it was easy to scare them! You didn't even have to do anything; a mere threat worked wonders. Egged on by liberal professors, students confronted administrators with lists of demands, deadlines, and threats of building takeovers. Quickly, authority collapsed into putty. Sensing this, the students reversed the whole order; instead of being the victims, they became the victimizers.

In May, one month after the uprising at Columbia University in New York, France experienced a near-revolution led by university students from the Sorbonne. Not only was the entire country racing toward the brink of revolution, but the entire world. Or so it did seem to American students. A sense of moral urgency seized those who, for years, had been patiently working through the system. Things were building up, and a climax was imminent.

In August 1968, along came the Democratic Convention in Chicago, and frustration exploded into violent confrontation. At first, the clubs wielded were not by idealistic youths, but by the police, whom the students had provoked. Tired of passive resistance and working through the system, and convinced that necessary reforms would never happen through conferences, symposia, organizing, demonstrations, or sheer good will, the students began fighting back. But the men in uniform were not scared university officials whom they could humiliate by locking in their offices and discussing their underwear in public. No, this time it was the real thing—police.

Kathy started out by throwing a stink bomb of butyric acid in the Palmer House in Chicago. Then she put on a fancy gown and made her way to the ladies' room where she lipsticked on mirrors, "Stop Murdering Vietnamese."

One thing was becoming apparent: action worked. Confrontation was more effective than reason. And the more dramatic the confrontation, the *less* reasonable, the faster the high. People needed their heads shaken up; their entire way of viewing the world had to be rattled before the revolution could take place. Polite seminars at Ivy League towers were jokes; dope and acid rock were the real catalysts for revolution. (Kathy personally opposed drugs or anything that tampered with her mind.) Street action was where it was at. Suddenly, you no longer had to be a college graduate; a hatred of authority was enough.

But there was a problem. Not everyone accepted this view. And so began a split within the once-unified nonviolent Students for a Democratic Society (SDS). Besides the Action Faction, those ready to seek an alliance with working class youth of America, there was another group, the Progressive Labor (PL) Faction. To the Action Faction, PL was a bore with its earnest methodical ways—a youthful version of the thirties' radicals who had rallied in Union Square, standing on milk cartons and talking to an audience of galoshes and babushkas. What did so grubby a group have in common with true American heroes? And when it came to taking risks, where were they? *Talking* revolution over coffee in cheap cafeterias. PL was a throwback to a dreary time in American history that had long since passed, sighed the Action Faction, with contempt.

Perhaps. But in accordance with stodgy, old-fashioned politics, PL was organized from above and loyal when it came to voting. No need to drop acid or blare rock music if you had blocks ready to support you when it came to the vote. And that is just what PL had—dutiful ranks who showed up to cast their ballot and who believed that by so doing, change would come one day.

Ugh! Pathetic echoes of parents, cried the Action Faction, who had a view of a world vastly different from the one their parents had known. And they intended to stress that difference visibly with a flamboyant sexuality and a name that had more in common with the outlaw, the bandit, the pirate, the vagabond—the mythic America upon which Hollywood had built its fortunes.

The Action Faction had had it with dour do-gooders. "We are tired of tiptoeing up to society and asking for reform. We're ready to kick it in the balls," declared Bill Ayers, a local Ann Arbor, Michigan organizer who was gaining notice, as was Diana Oughton, the woman he was then living with. Shortly after, the Ann Arbor Action Faction became the Jesse James Gang.

Not surprisingly, the Jesse James Gang did not have much respect for parliamentary procedure. Frontier antics were a more useful model. When the PLers at the University continued to organize around the school's defense contracts, the Jesse James Gang responded by threatening to beat them up. After all, what did the "grease," as the working class kids were called, care about university defense contracts?

In less than one month, the Jesse James Gang captured

66

control of the SDS chapter at Michigan University. But not before more than half its membership had been driven away.

However, that did not concern Ayers, Oughton, and their group. Desperadoes don't act in numbers guaranteed to fill a lecture hall; they act in gangs, four or five people willing to ride it out into the sunset.

Plans were made to form a youth culture. Leading the discussion was an SDS chapter from New York's Lower East Side, called Motherfuckers, after the line in black poet Le Roi Jones' poem, "Up against the Wall, Motherfucker." The Motherfuckers were hot stuff. They even made records. I bought one and remember listening to them chanting fuck-ing-suck-ing and not much more. But that was enough to suggest their politics.

Kathy, who had attended an SDS conference in Colorado as part of the Action Faction, stopped off in Chicago. With her was Diana Oughton, a Bryn Mawr classmate who had graduated two years before Kathy and had a roughly parallel political postcollege career, living with poor Indians in Peru before coming home to help start the Children's Community School (CCS) in Ann Arbor with Bill Ayers. Both she and Kathy had majored in foreign language and literature (Diana, in German), and both had spent time living in the countries they had first come to know through books. Both shared an active interest in children, and Diana was hoping to become pregnant. She wanted, along with Bill, to become a parent, although both were adamantly opposed to marriage, and Bill was opposed to monogamy. While teaching at CCS, he had even approached the mothers of some of his students.

Kathy and Diana paid a visit to a Bryn Mawr friend who was married to a professor of French at the university and who lived in a good neighborhood in the comfortable, middle-class style of intellectuals—a book-lined study, furniture of simple contemporary design, and a table of good wine and food. After they left, Kathy remarked, "The only people I know who live like this are friends of my parents."

To know what Kathy meant, all I have to do is think back to a party given on Cape Cod at roughly that time. The setting was a Wellfleet, oceanfront home, filled with the cream of the Cambridge/New York summer circuit. (Several present would later make guest appearances to Kathy in jail.) That evening they were going to decide how to end the war in Vietnam. After driving along the sweeping, pebbled drive, lit by the flashlights of children (who, like the women, served as charming little helpers), guests settled into a hammock or on a mat in the spare, Oriental-style main house. (The studio was off to the side a bit.) A map of an affluent suburb of Boston—Newton, as I recall—hung on the wall. There were holes to indicate, in the manner of visual aids, what would happen if Newton were bombed. How odd, I thought. Nobody present is *for* the war; on the contrary, everyone had been on all the marches, demonstrations, protests. (At that time, I had been working as the New York City coordinator for the Medical Committee for Human Rights, which provided medics on protest marches as well as the means for young college students to get out of the draft.) The men spoke as if they were world leaders holding a summit.

After the serious discussion, guests were invited to hear some poetry. Erica Jong was giving a reading in the dunes. An after-dinner cordial, of sorts, to the men who had carved out the main course.

Yes, Kathy's shit-detector system must have been at work in that Chicago apartment. Not only did her parents and their friends live like her Chicago host, they actually seemed intent on denying it. Again, a useful flashback. This time, a letter to a well-known, journalist civil libertarian, and friend of the Boudins, criticizing him for radical-chic posturing. In the course of the letter, I made a reference to his fancy co-op apartment. The next week a response appeared. Fancy co-op? Was I nuts? The letter-writer had looked up the journalist's address and found a listing for an apartment in a commercial area. True, there was one; it was his office. His co-op was unlisted, as was the summer home. But the letter-writer was convinced that the journalist, a champion of public institutions like schools (although he sent his own kids to private ones), could not possibly live in high style. Okay. People are entitled to their naïveté. But why didn't the champion of truth, justice, and free speech use his column to clarify matters, as he customarily does? I imagine it was because he knew the value of the image he projected, and he didn't want it tarnished. The hypocrisy of her Chicago pals was nothing new, and Kathy didn't waste time arguing with them.

By now 1968 was drawing to a close. The Students for a Democratic Society decided to call a national conference at the University of Michigan. High on the agenda was: What was the SDS position on blacks. The radicals adopted the Black Panther line that blacks were a separate people who should have a separate nation, while old reliable Progressive Labor saw blacks as workers like everyone else, except more so, what with the burden of discrimination added to the already-heavy worker burden. Even though they were the chief topic of debate at the meeting, the Panthers were not present. But their spirit was, and SDS adopted their radical position on blacks and the radicals' decision to become a youth party.

When the new year dawned, the Jesse James Gang felt it was time to test their ideas. In February they headed back to East Lansing, where, the previous year, SDS had held a convention with a special workshop in sabotage and explosives. The purpose was to draw off all spies and informants from the FBI and the police with the workshop so that the convention could go about its business relatively unnoticed.

The strategy worked. But undercover agents were not the only ones attracted to the special workshop. Sitting in with them was Cathy Wilkerson, who later, along with Kathy Boudin, was to escape the explosion set off by bombs in Wilkerson's father's town house.

The Gang's arrival in East Lansing coincided with a demonstration held on behalf of a radical psychology professor to whom Michigan State had refused to grant tenure because he gave As to all students. Bill Ayers fought with a cameraman from a Detroit TV station. Although no harm was done to the man, his camera was smashed and Bill was arrested. Diana's dividend check took care of the bail.

Meanwhile, Kathy Boudin became an author of *The Bust Book,* a "handbook" for "all political prisoners." "The cop and the judge wear different uniforms, but they seek to serve the same system we seek to destroy," she wrote in the introduction.

I was a graduate student at Brandeis, alma mater of Kathy's Chicago coconspirator, Abbie Hoffman, and Kathy's high school classmate, Angela Davis. I couldn't believe the groveling that went on among liberal white professors taking time out from their comfortably affluent lifestyle to join in the revolution. One professor actually begged to be allowed to hoist food up to the floor of the building that the blacks were holed up in after having seized it. Although he was spit upon, he continued to make offers—medicine, drugs, meetings, anything to be allowed a part. Then he went home, where he worried whether the liquor at a cocktail party honoring the revolution would spill onto the newly stained floors of his home.

Just as the university year was ending in June, an article called "The Weather Document" appeared in *New Left Notes.* Citing a line from the Bob Dylan song, "Subterranean Homesick Blues"—"You don't need a weatherman to know

70

which way the wind blows," the authors, two professors, said not only was it youths and blacks, but the entire world that was on the brink of revolution—Vietnam, Asia, Africa, Latin America. The time to act had arrived.

The excitement aroused by the document spread like wild-fire, and, in time, SDS called a convention in Chicago. By now the radical faction, known as The New Left or the National Office or National Collective, was called the Revolutionary Youth Movement or RYM (pronounced "rim"). After the convention, there were no phrases, no acronyms—one word replaced them all, and that word was Weatherman.

In addition to the young radicals at the conference, there were police with cameras photographing those in attendance. Police had a notorious record of harassing the Black Panthers, who posed with guns and assumed a military stance in general. This time the white radicals saw to it that Black Panthers were not only discussed and honored, but also were present. They understood that the Black Panthers had an appeal they never could have; they had the toughness born of real experience, having had to deal with police brutality all their lives. They were the natural street soldiers.

Panther Chaka Walls got up to speak. First he tossed some random insults at everyone. But before he was finished, he managed to focus on the newly emerging women's liberation movement. "We believe in the freedom of love, in pussy power," he declared.

"Fight male chauvinism," PLers yelled back.

"We have some puritans in the crowd. Superman was a punk because he never tried to fuck Lois Lane," Walls said.

Now this, remember, was the dawn of the seventies. Many political women were beginning to question the men's causes and concentrate on our own. With mirror, flashlight, and plastic speculum, we peeked inside ourselves, beginning our education where we all began—the womb. Movement-style

71

pamphlets were mimeographed, and one—*Our Bodies, Our Selves*—would subsequently go mainstream to become a bestselling book throughout the world.

Talk about our bodies led to talk about our men, many of whom would shortly become ex-s. For we were mad. We had marched for civil rights, for an end to the war in Vietnam, for all the things our men were for. But when you came right down to it, they treated us like cunts.

True. In Weathermen, women could assume leadership positions. But only if they also assumed the prone position recommended by black civil rights activist Stokeley Carmichael.

Now was the time for Kathy's shit detector system to go bonkers, for those who know her well describe her as an early and avid feminist. It should have lit up and sent out distress calls warning her not to fall into the trap set up by revolutionary honchos. Imagine calling us puritans for not remaining prone!

Why didn't Kathy split from the men guilt-tripping *us* for not going along with *their* so-called sexual revolution. I mean, you didn't even have to be female to recognize the bullshit. Even stodgy old PL picked up on it. Why, they hadn't been handed as golden an opportunity as that presented by Panther Walls in ages. And they wasted no time calling him on it. Fight male chauvinism, indeed!

But Kathy, it turns out, was more interested in "kicking ass"—the new action planned by Weathermen for Chicago in early October.

Kathy's decision to up the action ante should have been a signal for her father, who also comes equipped with a finely tuned set of antennae. Were I Leonard, sure, I'd have pride in Kathy's courage. Up until now her hijinks were not really violent, and they were for good causes. But I'd share Jean's concern about the flip side of such courage: self-destructiveness. And, if I knew about Kathy's kick-ass plan, I'd be worried. I mean, why's a brilliant kid joining up with white punks and street blacks to fight police in Chicago? That is, what did Kathy hope to accomplish besides some ventilation?

Yes, the street-learned fighting skills of black youths made them the urban equivalent of guerrilla soldiers in Latin America, but even Ché had said that guerrilla warfare in this country was doomed. But those damned kids! They weren't listening to anyone, not even their heroes. All they could think of was that tiny band of thirteen men Castro started out with and imagine that they were the same.

In August, Kathy left for Cuba with Diana Oughton and Ted Gold, both of whom would die shortly from bombs of their own making. Travel arrangements for the SDS delegation of thirty-six were tricky. The group left from several different cities with one-way air tickets to Mexico City, purchased from a Westchester travel agent. They planned to return to Canada by boat five weeks later.

Back in the States, the Black Panthers, of all people, came down hard on the Weathermen during a conference held on their own turf—Oakland, California. Weathermen had raided a PL caucus and beaten members, some badly enough to require hospitalization.

Reaction was immediate. David Hilliard, the highest-ranking Panther neither in jail nor exile, threatened Weatherman with physical violence. The Berkeley Radical Student Union denounced the beatings, and several members formed a new faction, RYM II, which would conduct an action of its own in Chicago.

Well, if the Black Panthers were going to act uppity, the Weathermen would turn to the grease, those working-class kids who had nothing to do but hang out at hamburger joints. And what better place to begin than a White Castle drive-in, in Detroit, where the Weathermen handed out a leaflet encouraging the youths to come to Chicago for the "Days of Rage," as kick-ass was renamed. It read, in part:

"The thing is this: The Man can't fight everywhere. He can't even beat the Vietnamese. And when other Vietnams start, man, he's just gonna fall apart. SDS is recruiting an army now, man, a *people's* army under black leadership that's gonna fight against the pigs and win!"

By now the women in Weatherman were beginning to gain a sense of themselves as soldiers but felt they needed some practice fighting as an all-female unit. As part of the SDS-Motor City Action, ten women decided to invade a class taking final exams at Macomb County Community College in Warren, Michigan and hand out a pamphlet on "SDS Women Fighters." The two men who protested were met with karate chops, and when the police came, the women fought back, but the police managed to arrest nine.

To the surprise of the Motor City 9, as they were quickly dubbed, they could not raise bail money in the leftist network of Detroit. Nevertheless, they managed to get out. By now, it was mid-August and the delegation from Cuba was returning. Bill Ayers left to meet them in St. John, Canada, and from there, it was on to Cleveland for a four-day Midwest National Action Conference where, for the first time, the role of women became the key issue.

Confident from separatist actions in the street and karate lessons, the women voiced what had up until now been the men's position: monogamy must go. Couples in love, the women said, defended each other in criticism sessions, something no revolution could afford. From that point on, there was to be no loyalty to individuals; all must go toward one end only—the Revolution.

The men did not argue, for in practice it was they who had

74

benefited from the smash-monogamy policy, previously called "foreskin privilege" by the women. Quick to pick up the political karma of the moment, Bill Ayers declared, "It's no longer that we can make posters about Vietnam with an old man and a little kid who are burned by napalm. The posters that we put out and the truth is the symbol of a woman with a gun. . . ." The truth, at least, for Bill Ayers and his female followers.

When the conference ended, seventy-five Weatherwomen drove to Pittsburgh, where they planned a practice run for Chicago. When they arrived, they asked the American Friends Service Committee if they could use their mimeograph machines. When they were refused, the women invaded the office and, holding workers captive, used the machines. With leaflets in hand, the women marched onto the ground of South Hills High School, spray-painting political slogans along their way. Once inside, they raced through the halls yelling "Jailbreak, shut down the school." The principal, already in shock from seeing one of the women open her blouse and thrust forth her breasts, rushed to call the police. When they arrived, the women fought the police the way they intended to do in Chicago. Taken by surprise, the police could not subdue the women, and several fought their way to freedom. Those who did not escape were arrested. This time their bail total was $56,000.

Bail money never proved a long-range problem; there was always someone who could cash a dividend check when support from the radical community dried up.

At about this time, the line from the Dylan song that had inspired the name Weatherman was modified to, "You don't need a rectal thermometer to know where the ass-holes are."

Such critical feedback seemed to spur the Weathermen on. Anyone who took criticism seriously was weak, except for self-criticism, which was carried on in the communes, along with karate, rifle practice, and certain deprivations intended to build up discipline. From time to time, for instance, members went for two to three days without sleep or two to three days without food. At other times, group sex was imposed. "People who fuck together fight together," declared Terry Robbins, who, self-conscious about the size of his penis, remarked, "It's not the size of the dog in the fight, but the size of the fight in the dog."

And women, intent on proving they were as free of middle-class hang-ups, proceeded to out-macho the men. One night Diana Oughton's collective killed, cooked, and ate a tomcat, and on another, they went around smashing gravestones in a local cemetery.

Raising money now became a problem. Some communes made plans to get cash by having both male and female members engage in prostitution. Diana Oughton was reported seen selling glassine bags of either heroin or coke. The main thrust now was to get rid of whatever remnants of bourgeois morality were left. Group sex, LSD, and homosexuality were ordered as part of a political platform to rid inhibitions and to weed out the police.

As the Days of Rage, October 8-10, approached, there was an anticipatory frenzy. But crowd estimates for Chicago, originally put at fifty to one hundred thousand, were quietly being reduced to a more realistic ten thousand, with some putting the figure—at its very worst—at twenty-five hundred.

Monday night, October 6, two days before the official start of the Days of Rage, a small group of organizers met in Chicago's Lincoln Park, where they dynamited a statue commemorating seven policemen killed by a bomb during a rally in Haymarket Square in the 1880s.

By Wednesday night, the official opening of the action, the Weathermen gathered with their helmets, clubs, and chains, ready to receive the thousands of high school grease and street blacks they expected. About three hundred, including themselves, showed up. Undeterred, the small group built fires from park benches, while a few stood up and spoke of Ché and white-skin privilege. Then with cries of world revolution echoing in the night air, the band of three hundred marched out of the park and headed for the Drake Hotel, where the presiding judge of the Chicago Seven Trial, Julius Hoffman, made his home. On the way to the Drake, the Weathermen started to attack police and passersby; one injured passerby turned out to be a friend of Diana Oughton's father, who had gone down to check on the safety of his car.

By ten o'clock, seventy Weathermen were under arrest; several had been badly beaten and three had been shot at.

The next day, Thursday, the women decided to show their strength. A group of seventy marched to Grant Park for the all-female action. Badly outnumbered by the police, they chanted "oink, oink, bang, bang, dead pig," as they tried to leave the park. Drop the long poles and remove the helmets, the police ordered. The women charged into the ranks. This time the police were prepared, and the women were overpowered and arrested.

A heated debate arose whether to proceed with plans for a march on Saturday. Fred Hampton, the head of Chicago's Black Panthers, had spoken out that very day at a RYM II rally. "We oppose the anarchistic, adventuristic, chauvinistic, individualistic, masochistic, and Custeristic Weathermen."

The Weathermen decided to proceed with the march. By the end of the day, 103 were under arrest and the rest were on the run. Still, the Weathermen claimed victory. Not a tactical one, they conceded, but a more important kind—a psychological win.

Bill Ayers was asked what the Weathermen were up to.

77

"Kill all the rich people. Break up their cars and apartments."

"But aren't your parents rich?"

Ayers conceded they were, adding, "Bring the revolution home, kill your parents, that's where it's really at."

At the end of the year in 1969, from December 27-31, Weatherman held its last open meeting in Flint, Michigan. Called the "war council," it was held in a Black dance hall decked out with cardboard pistols and paper mâché guns. It was sufficiently publicized to attract the interest of the Flint police and the FBI. Four hundred people showed up. Awaiting them were a sign, "Piece [guns] now," and a poster of Fred Hampton, who had denounced them in October and been gunned down by police December fourth in his own apartment.

Fred Hampton was not the only hero of the day. Referring to Manson, Bernardine Dohrn said, "Dig it, first they killed those pigs, then they ate dinner in the same room with them, then they even shoved a fork into a victim's stomach. Wild."

And for the rest of the war council, Weathermen held up three fingers, sign of the fork, when they greeted one another. Ted Gold, who was shortly to be blown to pieces in the town house explosion, remarked, "Well, if it will take fascism, we'll have to have fascism."

"We have to get into armed struggle," Dohrn argued. Mark Rudd, in an eerily prophetic statement, announced, "It's a wonderful feeling to kill a pig or blow up a building."

The war council ended just as the decade itself was coming to an end. A good time to take inventory. Which is what the Weathermen did. Everything in the Chicago headquarters; minutes of meetings, financial records, flyers and leaflets, pamphlets and posters, position papers, and mailing lists were to be destroyed. The seventies would start in a new way. Underground. Only those deemed worthy of the new urban army could stay on. That meant three of the four hundred had to go; the one hundred bravest would carry out the revolution.

Weathermen themselves joked that the first requirement for membership was a father who made at least thirty thousand dollars, although most would have had no problem passing the test had it been three hundred thousand. Weathermen understood that, up until the seventies, they had gotten off lightly; bail money was always available when needed and at worst they were sentenced to a month in jail. In contrast, black brothers like Fred Hampton were shot in their sleep by the police. (After thirteen years, in November 1982, Hampton's family won a settlement of 1.85 million dollars from city, county, and federal authorities for his death.)

No more "white skin privilege" for the newly organized army. The one hundred bravest divided itself into "affinity groups" composed of ten to thirty members that, in turn, broke into "cells" of four and five. Members moved out of old quarters and changed their hair; some dyeing it, others cutting it, and all abandoning flamboyancy. Henceforth, communications would take place through answering services and anonymous mail drops or post office boxes. The New York group called itself The Fork.

By the first week of March, one of its members made a trip to New Hampshire to purchase explosives, which were then driven to the The Fork's temporary headquarters, a solid town house, one in a row of historic Federal-style town houses on Eleventh Street, right off Fifth Avenue, three blocks from Washington Square Park in the heart of Greenwich Village. The house was owned by Cathy Wilkerson's father. While he was away on a vacation in the Caribbean, Kathy Boudin, Cathy Wilkerson, Diana Oughton, Ted Gold, and Terry Robbins took over his basement, which he had used as a workshop to restore antiques. They placed two cartons, each containing fifty pounds of dynamite, near his workbench, alongside the antipersonnel bomb Terry Robbins had been building, with plans to set it off at a Fort Dix Army dance.

On Friday morning, Diana had doubts about using bombs but was overruled by Terry, who pointed to his firebombing of the home of the judge presiding over the Panther 21 trial. No one, he said, had been killed. Diana, still shaky, went down to the basement to connect the wires to clocks. That way everyone would have time to get out safely before the explosion of weapons. Tired from lack of sleep, and inexperienced with weapons, Diana made a mistake. By noon all that was left of her that could be used for identification was a tip of a finger. Ted Gold and Terry Robbins also perished in the blast. Only Kathy Boudin and Cathy Wilkerson, who may have been in a bedroom or a sauna, made it out alive, Boudin naked and Wilkerson in jeans.

A neighbor, the then-wife of Dustin Hoffman, covered Kathy with a curtain that had been blown out by the blast, and another neighbor, who turned out to be the former wife of Henry Fonda, took both women in, let them use a shower, and gave them some old clothes. Kathy then went to her own family's town house a few blocks away where her mother commented about the town house explosion, making the point that they always put out the fires of the rich quickly. Then she asked if Kathy would be staying. Kathy said she did not know. When Jean got up the next day, Kathy was gone.

It would take another dozen years before Jean Boudin would see her daughter and then it would be behind bars when Kathy was in solitary confinement, having been indicted on thirteen counts of murder, robbery, and assault.

For the moment, the three violent town house deaths were hard enough on a pacifist, and Jean reacted by breaking down. How heartbreaking it must have been to realize that, had Kathy heeded her advice, the three might not have died and Kathy would not be hiding somewhere underground, forced to live out her life with memories of violence.

Leonard reacted differently. He tucked his fugitive daughter's picture inside his wallet and went about his business.

For a while, the Boudins seemed like a childless couple. In reality, there was their son. But he was not Kathy. He had chosen a much more conventional path, and although he walked it with distinction—Harvard Law School, *The Law Review,* clerking for a Supreme Court justice—he was clearly no rebel. And with such a relatively conservative and safe career, who could be sure he even approved of Leonard's any more than Leonard approved of his son's?

And there was something else. The son seemed more interested in establishing himself in a large prestigious law firm with lots of travel than in starting a family. In fact, when he later *was* established in one of the nation's largest corporate firms, teaching at Harvard, and holding Shakespeare readings at his home, he did become involved with an attractive, well-heeled woman. She reported the relationship lacked a future; Boudin's son was put off by her child from a previous marriage.

And Leonard, in keeping with the Left, was old-fashioned about family. Men should marry, and their bright attractive wives should bear them children.

In a short time, the Boudins resumed a normal life. Once again, their brownstone was home to the Left, and Leonard and Jean, as its first family, gathered a few distinguished young people, surrogate daughters and sons, of sorts. "They kind of adopted me," said a beautiful, brilliant "daughter," who was raising a son of her own, as Kathy would do. Like the real son, the surrogate had no children and was not married. But there was an important difference: although ambitious, he had no desire to become an establishment lawyer. He was a writer, and his book about Leonard's Harrisburg trial was so fine that Leonard had purchased several hundred copies.

But their was a complication. The surrogate son fell in love with a member of Leonard's defense team; yet he felt too unaccomplished to compete for her attention. He was not "a man of the world," as he quotes Leonard describing himself.

Nina, as I shall call the woman, was, in many ways, what Kathy might have been. Like Kathy, Nina was brilliant, beautiful, and a star athlete. She was also emotionally intense in a contradictory sort of way. She, too, had majored in a foreign language, French, at college and had taken some time out before making a major departure from Kathy's itinerary by entering law school. Upon graduation, Nina accumulated distinctions as an innovator the way Kathy had once done. But again, in sharp contrast to Kathy, Nina's innovations were in the area of women's rights.

I first met Nina in March 1970. Abortion was not yet legal, and we, along with thousands of other women, were marching to demand it become so. We both were wearing little white aprons; stamped on them in red was "Is this uterus the property of New York State?"

Nina was also wearing an engagement ring. It was made from an American plane downed in Vietnam, given to her by her fiancé, a dermatologist who had chosen to go to jail rather than train Green Berets in his specialty. Nina was proud of the ring; it was the same as that given to the Weathermen by the Vietnamese.

The symbolism was strong but the marriage was not. After his release from almost two years in prison, Nina's husband spurned offers to become the hero of the Left, choosing instead to improve the health of the poor, just as Jean had hoped Kathy would do. Shortly afterwards, Nina got a divorce.

Nina moved into the apartment of a black attorney/activist and together they wrote a landmark book on abortion. The two women traveled to France where they had an audience with the feminist "pope," Simone de Beauvoir. Nina's fluency in French made it easy to talk.

The next time our paths crossed was during the 1972 Democratic Convention in Miami. Again we were marching together for women's rights; Nina, her eyes burning and a banner raised, looked for all the world like a cross between Joan of Arc and Kathy Boudin, a look that landed her in the centerfold of the *Daily News*.

After the march, Nina changed into a long calico gown and matching bonnet, her costume for the movie being made about the convention. I was amazed at how easily Joan of Arc became Scarlett O'Hara, but then, Nina had always had a knack for switching back and forth from princess to warrior.

Later that summer, I bumped into Nina on Cape Cod. With her deep tan and tennis whites, she looked ready to take on the stars of the Cambridge/New York Left. She was living in an all-woman house owned by a *New Yorker* short-story writer who had gained his reputation by writing about the bittersweet emotions accompanying idolatry.

By the middle of the seventies, her career booming, Nina began taking her temperature at all-women get-togethers Having married an up-and-coming politician, she now fo cused all energy on one cause: conceiving a baby.

This was not unusual for women of extraordinary accomp lishments, especially pioneers like Nina. It's as if they needer an antidote to careerism, to the effort spent on "making it. The stress on achievement, the juggling of the personal an public, and the experimentation with alternative modes of living all called out for something simple and profound: the flesh of one's flesh. Shortly, Nina gave birth to a child of her own.

As always, Nina was a trend-setter. Within a few years, female stars of all sorts would be lusting after motherhood. Even Kathy Boudin.

But one thing was puzzling. A baby wasn't time out; Nina was calling it quits. She plunged into motherhood full time and even took up religion. Instead of being a lawyer, Nina, in a weird throwback to women of Jean's generation, married one, thus becoming a "wife of."

During her years as an abortion advocate, not all activists had supported Nina's struggle. Catholics and Orthodox Jews opposed it, of course; but so did the Black Panthers, who called abortion genocide, arguing that if blacks were to carve out a nation of their own, they needed an army, and for that they needed women to conceive black babies and carry them to term. Here their thinking happened to mesh with that of white male radicals who were for motherhood, although for different reasons. The sixties had produced a mythic figure, The Earth Mother, celebrated in folk song and other mellow aspects of pop culture. Along with her went birthing at home, usually on some commune with children, pets, and many bearded men. Birthing was in, right down to the placenta stew that was eaten in tribal fashion after it was separated from the newborn child and mixed with a little wine.

Weatherwomen, echoing the official party line of the men of the Black Panthers and those of the counterculture, agreed children were important, and most wound up becoming pregnant. There was a problem however: although their ideology was informed by the Panthers and other self-proclaimed radical groups, their goal was to work with "the people," and "the people" had a different notion of children. To begin with, it included family and that meant marriage.

But Bill Ayers and Diana Oughton, whose progressive school for black children in Ann Arbor had the motto "Children Are Only Newer People," did not believe in marriage. "How can anyone do anything so thoroughly conventional and bourgeois and limiting as get married?" Diana said, when a friend asked if she was planning to get married after Diana told her she might be pregnant.

Also, Bill and Diana were not concerned about teaching children how to read or preparing them for good schools and good jobs—the predominant concerns of the black parents who had chosen to send their children to the unconventional progessive school.

Bill Ayers had no need to worry about anything as bourgeois as making a living. His father was chairman of the Commonwealth Edison Company of Chicago and a trustee of Northwestern University. Dividend checks saw to it that Bill was covered for anything, including bail. As Bill himself put it, "If he [his father] wants to finance the revolution, that's okay with me." Bill jokingly referred to his parents as "Ma and Pa Power-brokers."

With the same sense of entitlement that made Bill feel he did not have to concern himself about money (others had already done that for him), he also felt he did not have to respect anyone's wishes for sexual loyalty. Although it was politically "correct" among young radicals to oppose monogamy, many of the women still found this difficult to accept when they were living with a man.

Diana told a friend about a time she had left Bill in Ann Arbor for five days. When she returned, she learned that he had slept with a different woman every night she had been away, and one hundred in three months. Diana said she tried to remind herself that this was the way it was supposed to be, but when she thought about it, she could not help but feel hurt.

Of course, such attitudes about marriage and running

85

around with a different woman every night were not the sort of thing to put an upwardly mobile black family, anxious to escape cultural stereotypes, at ease.

Equally disturbing to the black parents who had enrolled their children in the Community Children's School (CCS) was the fact that they weren't learning how to read and, hence, would not be able to get into any college, let alone a top one that would lead them up the ladder of success that Ayers and Oughton were trying so hard to climb down. In time, funding for the school and the energy necessary to keep it going atrophied.

The grease were not exactly bowled over either. To begin with, trying to recruit working-class white youths into their army was a denial of another reality: poor youths, both black and white, were being recruited and drafted into a real army. One, because it paid; and two, because they had no choice. There were no liberal groups setting up draft-counseling centers in ghetto areas the way they did in areas that served white college students.

Besides, street-wise kids know there's a difference between a rich college kid who lives off dividends from daddy and themselves. They know that when they go to jail, they are not automatically bailed out. They also do not publicly politicize their rage. Not at the family, at least. Working-class youths may have as much anger at their parents as the Weathermen had and as much need to rebel, but they do not have parents who continue to support them no matter what they say or do. It is unthinkable to an average, working-class youth to say "bring the revolution home, kill your parents, that's where it's really at." Working-class kids have not had the luxury of announcing their murderous plans on public platforms. If anything, such violent talk would be greeted with violence. To speak out against the family incurs a fear of retaliation. Authority to the working-class young is not benign; that is why they hate it.

Of course, if you spent your time, as sixties radicals did, shuttling back and forth between "the people" and delegates from revolutionary governments of foreign nations, it would probably be hard to get a good fix on reality.

But again, the working class wasn't doing this shuttling number, and hence, they never developed any sense that they could impose their way of thinking on the masses of the world in the name of Revolution. Life was immediate— getting through each day on one's own turf. Delegates from provisional governments were as abstract to the grease as not being able to cough up bail money for drunken driving would be to an SDSer.

It was not enough for the Weathermen to renounce their class origins by showing contempt for everything most of the grease would give their lives to own. As would their black brothers.

By the end of the sixties, black men were beginning to catch on to honky's hypocrisy. To express their indignation, they started talking about rape. Diana Oughton took note. When visiting a friend near a black section of Chicago, she first inquired about safety. "You don't know how much anger there is in a black man," she said.

But it wasn't the black man's anger that would do her in; it was her own. Shortly before the town-house explosion, Bernardine Dohrn had spoken with an awe-struck approval of dining off the corpses of freshly killed victims. After Diana was demolished, Dohrn seemed to have a change of heart.

"The deaths of three friends ended our military conception of what we are doing.... We went back to how we had begun, living with groups of friends, and found that this revolution could leave intact the enslavement of women if women did not fight to end and change it together...," she wrote in a letter published in *Rat,* December 1969/January 1970 issue.

In the early seventies, it seemed as if Kathy, too, chose a

87

quieter life. How much of this choice was voluntary is hard to say, for the Weathermen had "demilitarized" their units. Kathy, who had consistently favored an escalation of violence in her Eleventh Street cell, The Fork, was removed from a position of leadership.

Those "into" action would now have to settle for symbolic bombing. Only three months after the town house explosion, the New York City Police Headquarters was bombed, but no one was hurt. Most of the Weathermen and other underground activists moved about freely. In her autobiography, *Growing Up Underground,* Jane Alpert describes going to a roof with friends to watch a bomb she had planted shortly before go off.

Assuming a new physical identification was easy but no longer enough. For the first time there was a need for new names, and the Weathermen assumed aliases and false IDs. Also necessary were places where the fugitives could live while in hiding. And so a network of "safe houses" was established, some in cities and others on rural communes. Transportation was mainly by public means in the city. Fugitives took subways to the end of the line, and then, leaving in different taxis, drove separately to destination points a few miles away, before taking a bus ride back. Not once did they return to a place they had been at before going underground.

Some of the Weathermen left the country altogether, a few winding up in Canada. Those who had settled there to avoid the draft helped the fugitives with their IDs for border crossings. Others went to Cuba. But mainly it was the network of radical, affluent activists, writers, artists, and Leftist lawyers, who harbored the fugitives in their homes.

For those who could not abandon the romance of revolution, the creation of an army of outlaws held an immediate appeal. In September 1970, the Weathermen arranged for

Timothy Leary to escape from a California prison where he was serving time for possession of marijuana. To sympathizers, this was heroics worthy of Robin Hood himself, especially since it was not publicized that the Weathermen demanded twenty thousand dollars to release the sixties guru.

By the seventies, Weathermen had participated in actions on the Pentagon and other symbols of the military, but somehow the spark that had ignited the Days of Rage was gone. For one, the Vietnam War was no longer popular at home and Nixon was already on his way out.

By the mid-seventies, many of the fugitives were having second thoughts about their life underground. It was joyless and drab and lacked the momentum that had swept them forward in the sixties. Now, instead of confrontation and street action, there were menial jobs and the ever-present worry of being caught. Kathy Boudin was said to be living in Boston where she worked as a hospital aide while once again contemplating medical school.

As with grounded squid, which ejaculate an inky spurt before they become transparent and die, the Weathermen had their premortem release. In 1974, the Weathermen published a book-length pamphlet called *Prairie Fire*. It was printed by gloved hands to avoid fingerprints and released underground.

In 1974 Jane Alpert gave herself up to authorities, becoming the first underground fugitive to surface. Then one by one, as the decade progressed, the others followed her example. By the time the eighties dawned, just about all the Underground fugitives had surfaced, with one exception—Kathy Boudin.

In 1975, while still underground, the Weathermen published a magazine called *Osawatomie,* in which they claimed that the Weather Underground had carried out twenty-five bombings. Although injuring no one, they were not quite symbolic gestures. One bomb cracked the walls of the Capitol building, while another blew out the dust on Center Street, the police headquarters. But the publication was not all politics; also included were poetry, short stories, and nonfiction about life on the run. One cell reported its members had managed to infiltrate an antibusing group in Boston.

That same year, three filmmakers made the movie *Underground*. In it, Kathy Boudin, Cathy Wilkerson, Bill Ayers, Bernardine Dohrn, and Jeff Jones were filmed through a gauzy, protective haze; in theaters around the country, movie-goers had a chance to watch them as well as to hear what they had to say about their life underground.

Kathy, asked about the town house explosion, spoke in abstract, almost literary, terms. Quoting from a poem, "what it feels like to be inside an explosion," Kathy says, "It's that kind of time that can't be counted on a clock. It's that kind of time that seems to go on forever. And you have a chance to see your whole life in that moment and also the lives of your friends."

Jeff Jones, who was not there, spoke of the explosion in a very different way, describing how the survivors had to walk over a collapsed floor that had fallen twenty feet; how it was pitch black with dust everywhere, and how everyone had only one thing in mind—escape. And once they did get out, everyone headed for the subways, going under turnstiles two at a time and then, emerging from the subway, panhandling above ground.

Of course, the truth is neither as abstract as Kathy's description nor as grimy as Jones's. Kathy did not scurry to a subway and duck under a turnstile. Kathy went to a neighbor's home, took a shower, got some clothes, and headed for her own family's town house a few blocks away.

Kathy does, however, state that it was amazing to ride the

subways days later and watch people read about her in the papers, when she knew all along that they couldn't find her. Writing in *Mademoiselle,* Ellen Cantarow says her words suggest some "thrilling sense of invincibility," even "omnipotence." Even in prison Boudin writes as if she is entitled to all the amenities of civilized living, forgetting entirely that she is there as an accused murderer.

Boudin returns to the themes of compressed time in a poem she wrote for Joanne Chesimard, also known as Assata Shakur.

The poem is in "sing a battle song poems by women in the weather underground organization." The title surrounds a mask and inside there is a note of explanation: "COVER: This spirit mask is in celebration of our sister, Diana, who spent several years of her life in Guatemala." It does not mention how the "sister" ended her life. A little note also accompanies the poem called "For Assata Shakur." It says, "Written on the night of the bombing of William Bundy's office in the MIT Research Center, done by the women's Proud Eagle Tribe." It is dated June 1973, roughly one month after Chesimard's capture by New Jersey State Troopers, May 2, 1973. And according to the note at the end of the poem, "[she] faces charges including murder, assault, and armed robbery. Here is the poem in its entirety:

> Underground is not the right word
>     it makes it seem too simple
> as if there is an easy way to disappear
>     a place to go —
> Beneath the city streets
> there is no safe passage.
> You moved among your people
>     in a gentle wind
> Invisibility winding into their lives

Constrained a normal human response to daily
   injustice
   with an exhausting effort
A ballooning beneath of anger caged inside
Carefully choosing the moment of attack
And the earth turns with a racing rhythm
   running the guerrilla
      through the changes of a normal lifetime
      in a single month
And when you were captured, sister
   I wept
      for all of us.

By 1978, three years after the film *Underground* had been shot, the Weather Underground broke into two factions—the Prairie Fire Collective and the May 19th Coalition. Members of the Prairie Fire Collective advocated surfacing. In it were Bernardine Dohrn, Bill Ayers, and Cathy Wilkerson.

During that same year, Kathy Boudin moved into the three-bedroom co-op then occupied by Rita Jensen and her teenage daughters. Jensen, thirty-five, had been a welfare mother although at the time of Boudin's arrest, she was working as a reporter for the Stamford Advocate. Jensen had been on welfare while a student at the Columbia School of Journalism. Boudin, using one of her aliases, was still receiving welfare at the time of her arrest, although the address was so unlikely that one of the co-op members tried to mail back a check, certain it had arrived by mistake.

Shortly before her move into the old, established co-op building, Boudin accused members of the Weather Underground of being bourgeois. She and a few others formed the Revolutionary Committee, which was busted by the FBI. It was after the bust that the remaining fugitives from the Underground surfaced; among them, Mark Rudd, nominal leader of the Columbia uprising; Bernardine Dohrn; and Cathy Wilkerson, the other survivor of the explosion in the town house owned by her father. Wilkerson was the only one given time—three years for possession of dynamite.

Then, in May 1979, the FBI decided to call it quits, as if the end of the decade signaled the end of the chase. For almost ten years they had been searching for members of the Underground. Now nine had surrendered willingly, several citing, as reason, children. In 1980, Boudin became a mother too. Still, Kathy would not give herself up. Instead, she registered for welfare under the alias of Lydia Adams, calling her child Chesa, but giving his name as C. Jackson Adams to officials. Ironically, she had said in the movie *Underground* that being a welfare mother is like being in captivity and "you need to have other people to help you." And there were. For one, the government helped out Lydia Adams by sending her $177.75 every two weeks.

What is one to make of Kathy's preference for a double identity, even when no longer hounded by the law. It suggests the loner, again the voice from the underground (and from Russian literature). The only one who does not give herself up. And yet Kathy wanted to lead the normal life of a mother; more than anything else, it is time with Chesa that she now misses. Her neighbors in the co-op describe her as an extremely loving and devoted mother. Yet, they also describe another Kathy Boudin, the Kathy who is not with Chesa, the woman who glowers at them with angry, intense eyes. Or the "cold fish," as a former political ally put it; or the woman who was "intimidating," as Jane Alpert described her.

I suspect that Kathy Boudin could not be an equal in a group, although she ardently believed she ought to be. But

Kathy Boudin is a divided woman. She can be a leader in a group, as she was in the Underground, or a follower, as she was with the black leaders.

According to Alpert, Kathy was in love with a woman. She told Jane "her experience of both dominance and submission with her lover had been as intense as in her affairs with men." When Jane saw her in Boston in 1974, the affair had just ended, and she reports that Kathy was heartbroken. Jane, who was visiting a mutual friend, entered the apartment and saw a woman sitting in a rocking chair. She did not turn around. Jane went up to her.

"You know who I am?"

Jane said she did not.

"I'm Kathy Boudin."

In her book, Jane says she felt intimidated the whole time. She didn't know if Kathy was trying to seduce her or intimidate her or both.

Alpert had argued with Kathy that "intimacies with women tended to be equal." Kathy couldn't accept that. As she had just said, domination and submission ruled her relationship with either sex. Consistent with that was her choice of becoming a member of the May 19th Coalition where she became a subordinate of black men in charge of the revolution. Using her "white skin privilege," in a parody of old-fashioned roles, Kathy the female would rent cars and sit up front, looking demure; and the men, armed blacks, would carry out the actual violence.

And then she would go home and in a cooperatively run, woman-headed household, Kathy would raise her son, becoming Kathy Boudin, Superwoman, a synthesis of guns and motherhood, unable to recognize any contradiction in her dual roles.

For a die-hard revolutionary who couldn't concede defeat, the May 19th Communist Organization was the perfect answer. Here was a fusion of the sixties' concern with class and race—poor black criminal men replacing white college men—and the seventies' concern with women's independence. For although the May 19th Communist Organization was dedicated to ending imperialism by armed struggle, it was organized as an all women's group.

Boudin, Clark, and her attorney, Tipograph, are all members of the May 19th Communist Organization. It has published a booklet called *Liberation in Our Lifetime*. It is not some internal memo; it is an appeal to members of the women's liberation movement. I purchased it in a bookstore for a dollar. On the cover are two pictures: the top shows Third World women marching in army uniform, rifles held close to their bodies. Then comes a subtitle, "A Call to Build a Revolutionary Anti-imperialist Women's Liberation Movement. May 19th Communist Organization."

May 19, by the way, is the birthday of Malcolm X, Ho Chi Minh, and Kathy Boudin. (Coincidentally, it is also the birthday of Lucy Madeira, founder of the Madeira School, where Jean Harris served as headmistress before she shot the Scarsdale Diet doctor. The school, the alma mater of Diana Oughton, celebrated May 19 with fresh strawberries. (It was also, by chance, on May 19, 1982, that Bernardine Dohrn started the eight-month jail sentence imposed on her for refusing to cooperate in the Brink's investigation. Dohrn was the woman who, after Diana's death, moved in with Ayers, taking care of Kathy's child, Chesa, along with her own two young children.)

The first part of the booklet is primarily a celebration of women around the world struggling against imperialism by forceful (called revolutionary) means. In a section called "liberation through participation," there are pictures of "ZANIA women freedom fighters at bayonet drill," all about to lunge forth with long weapons. (A Freudian would have a field day with penis envy.) Then we get slightly closer to home with a section on "Black Women Under U.S. Imperialsim." It is when we reach the section called "White Women and Imperialism" that I wonder where these women have been.

The antipornography movement, described under a picture showing two white women involved with target practice, is one where, we're told, "the government and police have waged a campaign to get white women to ally with the police as the way to fight the rise of violence against women. By calling for more police protection, 'Take Back the Night' *and the entire state-led anti-rape movement appeals to the armed forces of the imperialist state. . . ."* [Emphasis, mine.] Does this explain the brutality, humiliation, and indifference that women who have been beaten or raped report as their experience? How many black women favor rape? Or are willing to wait until the revolution to see its end?

But this just begins the attack. "Such a movement," says the booklet, "must be destroyed." They do not mean the white power elite; it is the women's liberation movement that is the target. And then to reinforce their position, they proceed to describe how white women at the conference were being recruited by the Klan (which they say was "admitted as a legitimate minority opinion"), along with the CIA, FBI, and multinational corporations.

I was at the Houston conference representing New York State as an unofficial (nonvoting) delegate. I can still remember the glares of men as we filed into the massive auditorium and the comments about dikes and chicks and anything else the men felt free to toss at the women. I remember one delegate, a middle-aged Midwesterner representing rural farm women, changing her mind about the rights of lesbians. It was based on her first experience with male harassment on the street. "You just don't find that sort of thing at the farm," she said.

96

It is true the conference planners and some liberal supporters like Betty Friedan had hoped that the two most controversial issues, abortion and lesbianism, would not have
time to be voted on. Hence they were put at the end of the
alphabetically arranged agenda. (Abortion was under "R"
for reproductive freedom; lesbianism was one notch further
down under "S" for sexual preference.) The more frightened
liberals wanted the agenda to stop at E. When the vote to
support the ERA was passed late Saturday night, there was
dancing in the aisles, and Bella Abzug told us all to go home
and have a good night's rest. But *she* did not stop there. We
had another day of debate to get to the end of the alphabet.

By the time we reached the most controversial issue, lesbianism (abortion was controversial but, in contrast, had gone
public many times), one woman from each delegation went to
receive the balloons stating "We Are Everywhere," ready to
rise in unison if the vote on lesbianism passed. And it did.

So it came as some surprise to read the booklet's totally
distorted description of the Houston conference, not only
because of its outright lies but because it follows their view of
the way lesbians, in particular, suffer in a male supremacist
society because they "challenge women's dependent and
subservient role in this society . . . and they identify with
other women rather than with the system of male su-
premacy."

(It is an irony that the analysis in this manifesto is politically consistent with many of the assumptions of the male
Left *except* that of sexual preference. The male Left fears
lesbians. Suppose more women choose to make love with
women than men. That would not only rob men of their
leadership role, but omit them altogether from lovemaking
with women.)

Then on to more attacks on women's liberation leaders,
particularly the one who has come the closest to bridging

KATHY BOUDIN AND THE DANCE OF DEATH

gaps among very different groups of women all over the country and the world, Gloria Steinem.

Then it's back to the solution of the women of May 19th—a call to arms, "More than just survive, we must build our capacity to fight."

To see the May 19th manifesto translated into action, let's "cut" to mid-Manhattan. It is three o'clock on a Saturday afternoon. Christmas is approaching and the area is filled with shoppers. Macy's and Gimbels are only a few blocks from the mail drop on West Thirty-second Street. But shoppers are not the only people in the area; for ten days law enforcement officials have been waiting at West Thirty-second Street, waiting for someone to pick up the mail.

On the tenth day a woman with carrot-red hair appears. The officers watch her open the box; then they move in. The woman refuses to give information; the police arrest her anyway. They have information enough.

Cut again. This time to a secluded ranch high in the mountains near San Francisco. It is called Wellspring, 130 acres. For years, say police, the incorporated commune has served as a weapons training ground for radical groups: the Black Panthers, the Symbionese Liberation Army, and the Weather Underground. Officials believe the commune, home to a San Francisco radical group called Tribal Thumb, was connected to the Manson Tribe.

One day Roseann Guston, a twenty-seven-year-old woman who had been part of Wellspring decides she has had enough. She and a friend gather their belongings and set out to leave. They make it five miles out of the commune when they come upon two other women, Judy Abramson and Wendy Sue Heaton. Abramson and Heaton do not want Guston and her friend to leave. So Heaton forces Guston to her knees and holds her down on the ground. Abramson gets out her gun and shoots her in the head. Guston's friend runs to get help.

98

When she returns, Abramson and Heaton are gone; only Guston is there, lying on the ground, blood gushing from her head. Her friend manages to get her to a hospital. Doctors try to save her, but the damage from the gunshot cannot be stemmed. Two days later, Guston dies.

Guston's father, a legislative aide to California State Senator Jack Gordon, initiates an official investigation. Police raid the mountain ranch. All the members have fled.

Cut again. This time to a clerk in a small office in Jacksonville, North Carolina, where births and deaths are registered. The clerk has received a request for the birth certificate of a Sharon Jarrell. She goes to get it; that's odd, she thinks. Why would anyone want it now? Sharon Jarrell was born in 1953; she would be twenty-nine, had she lived. But Sharon Jarrell did not make it through the first day of her life, according to her death certificate. And yet someone is requesting her birth certificate twenty-nine years later. The clerk thinks about it and then remembers a memo the office received from the FBI, issued after the Brink's shootout. It had warned all bureaus of vital statistics to be alert for odd requests, the kind that had previously gone unnoticed and made it possible for Boudin and Clark and other women involved with Brink's to obtain false IDs which, in turn, enabled them to rent cars and use aliases backed by credit cards.

The clerk contacted the officials. The letter with the request for the dead baby's certificate had a return address: Miller Associates, 134 West Thirty-second Street, New York, N.Y.

The woman with the carrot-red hair turned out to be Betty Abramson, wanted in the June 1981 murder of Guston. Abramson wasn't talking. But a police officer who had searched Marilyn Buck's East Orange, New Jersey, "safe" house remembered a photograph he had found there. It bore a striking resemblance to Abramson. Officials then tried to find links between Abramson and Brink's. In the course of their search, they came upon a radio transmitter, a radio base station, hidden in the Bronx apartment that had served as a safe house for the Brink's suspects, which, in turn, was traced through the Federal Communications Commission to the Wellspring Commune.

Abramson was held on a half-million dollars bail and sent to the Metropolitan Correction Center, which at the time also housed Kathy Boudin and Judy Clark. It would not be until the spring that Abramson's partner, Wendy Sue Heaton, would be apprehended in New Orleans, walking with *her* baby—an eleven-month-old daughter, and one year later that both women would plead guilty to a manslaughter charge.

What is the background of a woman who adheres to the philosophy of the May 19th Organization? The professional life of Susan Tipograph, the attorney for Judy Clark, can be used to chart the journey from the macho male Left to a macho female Left.

Like the thousands of other Jews who left Eastern Europe in search of freedom from persecution, Tipograph's parents immigrated to this country. In the old country, the men had been in the printing business; here, in the new country, her father became a businessman on his own; and her mother worked in a doctor's office. Shortly after Susan was born, the family gained sufficient mobility to move from Brooklyn to Teaneck, New Jersey. After her graduation from American University in 1972, Susan went on to New York Law School.

In 1973, Susan, still a law student, began working with the Attica Brothers Legal Defense Fund. But it was her work with the Puerto Rican independence movement that gave her a place in the pantheon of Leftist legal stars.

In 1979, Willie Morales, the FALN (Puerto Rico Independence Movement) leader, had his hands blown off while making bombs. "Tip," as his lawyer was called, filed suit against the New York City Department of Correction, demanding they move Willie from Riker's Island Hospital to Bellevue. Tip argued that Morales was being denied medical treatment at Riker's. Tip won her case and Morales was moved to Bellevue.

Shortly afterwards, Morales cut through the iron-mesh grate on his cell window with smuggled wire cutters and shimmied down three flights to the ground using Ace bandages as his chute. Police say Tip was the last person to have a contact visit with Morales. After that, Tip discovered, the FBI was following her twenty-four hours a day. She became an expert in the laws of electronic surveillance as well as search and seizure.

For four years the FBI continued to search for Morales. Then in early June 1982, as the Brink's federal trial was in process, he was captured in Puebla, Mexico, after a shootout that left one policeman and one FALN member's companion dead.

The following week an FALN member turned informant. In a sentencing memorandum filed against five FALN members, a white female attorney was said to have passed Morales a set of bolt cutters. The attorney had argued that the attorney-client privilege protected her from routine prison search, and guards let her slip past unsearched. That attorney is said to be Tipograph, although she insists those accusations are nothing but "lies."

According to the informant, the May 19th Communist Organization helped with the escape, as did the Black Liberation Army, which had armed teams in the area of Bellevue Hospital at the time of Morales's escape.

A further Brink's connection surfaced in the memo: Julio Rosado, one of the five FALN supporters whose legal advisor was Susan Tipograph, left fingerprints in the Pittsburg safe house rented by Nathaniel Burns, one of Kathy's initial codefendents in the Federal Brink's trial. (As the only remaining non-fugitive defendant indicted on both state and federal levels, Burns's state charges have been dropped.)

Tip lives with two other women. It is a coincidence that they all have the name Susan; it is not a coincidence that they all have similar political views. During the Morales trial, Tip and one other roommate, Susan Rosenberg, who has since been indicted in connection with Brink's, were arrested for assaulting a court officer. Tip pleaded guilty to the charge. Tip and her other roommate, Susan Rautenberg, worked together on the 1979 legal defense of their friend J. J. Johnson, who was convicted of attempting to murder a police officer.

Then things changed, and Tip started to work for women. She became the lead counsel for Judy Clark, Eve Rosahn, and six other women in a hundred-million-dollar lawsuit brought against Richard Nixon and his aides for using illegal means—wiretaps, mail openings, and burglaries—to gather evidence against the women for the Chicago Days of Rage demonstrations. She also was the attorney for Rosahn on a charge that she threw acid at a police officer at Kennedy Airport on September 26, 1981 (barely a month before Nyack), to protest the arrival of the South African rugby team, the Springboks.

Rosahn was subsequently jailed for refusing to cooperate with officials investigating her alleged role as an accomplice in Brink's.

In 1982, Tip won an out-of-court settlement on the wiretap case. The money was used to bail out another alleged Brink's accomplice, Sylvia Baraldini, one of the founders of the May 19th Communist Organization. At the time of her arrest, she was employed by Tip as a legal assistant.

Tip has other personal/political connections to the women involved with Brink's. Buck, allegedly "the only white member of the Black Liberation Army," had been sentenced to a ten-year term for gunrunning for the BLA. Tip was the person Buck was visiting when she disappeared on a furlough from Federal prison in 1977, according to authorities.

There was a time in the late sixties and early seventies when many a Jewish male Leftist in his twenties and thirties tried to resemble Fidel Castro. No coincidence. Cuba was an early inspiration to the male Left of a violent revolution that worked. It is an irony that Castro, an inspiration to the Left, put homosexuals in prison, an irony because many of the women connected with the newly named Springboks Seven are both ideologically, and in practice, lesbian. Of course, Leftist lawyers, like Kunstler, are not used to being ousted sexually, so they accused Tip of being tough and being too close to her clients, even though Kunstler offered Jerry Rubin, a one-time Kunstler client, the use of his New York City pad in his absence.

When the *Soho Weekly News* profiled Tipograph, Kunstler was quoted as saying, "Susan's dedication to her clients is immense. She loves the people she represents."

But Kunstler, a radical when it comes to blacks, a radical when it comes to the poor, a radical when it comes to those being harassed by government, is nonetheless a man. Like his colleague Leonard, he is a hero, a star, an idol. Women like Tip do not put him at ease. "As you get deeper into her, the intensity will frighten you and turn you off," he says.

This is not the first time the Left has been "turned off" by women who feel intensely about issues. Although its spokesmen know how to couch their objections to strong women in elegant ideologies, their endorsement of strong women is contradictory.

One way to deal with a double bind or contradiction is to adopt a rigid attitude, to make everything black or white, to eliminate all possible sources of confusion. I believe that

Tipograph and Clark chose this method to deal with a dual position that could lead to madness. They sought to live their lives in accordance with what they believe and to try to eradicate the gap between the personal and political—a feminist ideal, to be sure.

But the tragedy is that Clark and Tip and the other women in their circle did not challenge the male Left's premises. They, too, believe that the root source of oppression is class, and that once that is eliminated, the revolution is won. Somewhere they must have known that men are the problem, too; why else would they be organizing a women's movement? But a women's movement, no matter how 100 percent pure female it is, is not a women's liberation movement if it is organized around the principles of violence, struggle, and conquest.

The radical women involved with Brink's worked within a network established by the male Left. Part of it revolved around Lincoln Hospital, where I worked. At that time, the Young Lords, a Puerto Rican group fashioned after the Black Panthers, were active. Working with white Leftists, they planned to organize the South Bronx into a people's guerrilla army composed of young street Hispanics. But they had a problem; most were on drugs. Hence, the formation of the detoxification program where the new high was to be political organizing. For many, it was. Buildings were seized, offices taken over; there were sit-downs, lists of demands, and negotiations with frightened and ignorant white bureaucrats—a kind of update of the sixties campus takeovers. During this time, many of the leaders had their first exposure to the media. One particularly effective leader, Felipe Luciano, became an equally effective TV reporter. Another, a white psychiatrist, became a filmmaker and moved to the redwood forests of California. It was an intense time, and many dropped out when the drama ebbed. Others stayed to work in the poor area so desperately lacking in medical services.

And herein lies another Leftist network with surprising ties to the characters in the Brink's cast.

Alan Berkman, who worked at Lincoln Hospital, is the doctor who performed an abortion for Judy Clark after her arrest, a variation of another sixties phenomenon when it was common for the white Leftist doctors with whom I worked, to vie for the honor of delivering the baby of a Black Panther's girlfriend. I remember one, in particular, who has since gone on to become a sex therapist, boasting that he was going to deliver the baby of Afeni Shakur, fathered by a Black Panther.

Mutulu Shakur is believed to be the "brains" behind the Brink's robbery. According to the FBI, part of roughly one million dollars stolen in a series of holdups and shootouts was used to maintain a Harlem acupuncture clinic Shakur helped start. The clinic is called BAANA, the Black Acupuncture Association of North America. According to the information provided by a confidential source, Samuel Brown, the activists met at the clinic the morning of October 20. The clinic, it is believed, was the headquarters and communications center for the Brink's suspects. Several of the parking tickets belonging to the tan Honda that crashed into the wall in Nyack after the robbery were issued in the area of the clinic. The Honda was registered to Eve Rosahn, one of Tip's clients in the suit against the FBI for illegal surveillance.

In keeping with the thinking of the sixties, Shakur believed that drugs, like abortion, were part of the country's plan to do away with blacks. Or in the revolutionary parlance, it was part of the imperialist strategy of genocide. Lincoln Hospital, pressured by white liberal doctors and Puerto Rican street activists who formed a rainbow coalition (Chinese people

105

and native Americans were included), had started a drug detoxification program. One of the founders of the Lincoln Detoxification Program was Michael Tabor, one of the Panther 21 indicted, along with Weems and Burns, for plotting to plant bombs in department stores and murder cops. All were later acquitted.

With enthusiasm, skills, and political commitment, (all abysmally lacking when Lincoln had been the guinea pig hospital of Albert Einstein School of Medicine), the detox program received $750,000 from the City although it was no secret that Lincoln Detox was also a haven for radicals. Jennifer Dohrn, sister of then-Weather Underground woman Bernardine, worked there. At the time, Jennifer Dohrn and Judith Clark were living together in Greenwich Village. The FBI was on the lookout, requesting personnel files and tapping telephones. This made for an atmosphere of paranoia. Fed up with continual searches, Lincoln Detox created its own security staff.

Many addicts in the South Bronx were cured of their addiction by acupuncture skillfully administered. Hence, hospital administrators, relieved that they no longer had to worry about their own staff members being attacked by addicts, did not want to shut down the program despite its political activities.

In 1976 Lincoln Hospital opened a new building; gone were the dungeonlike conditions (the hospital had been built for runaway slaves) and the long empty alleyways and old stairwells with their easy access to clinical quarters. Detox, however, continued to act as if it were independent from the hospital. In 1977 the city asked to audit Detox's records but was told they were private. Elected officials were quoted as saying Detox "had a well-documented record of millions of dollars in unsubstantiated payroll costs."

In May of 1978, Lincoln Detox was ended. Koch had the

New York City police surround the building on the day of the ouster.

Lincoln Detox left Lincoln and set up quarters in a satellite clinic nearby. Nine months later, Shakur left the Bronx altogether and set up shop in Harlem. With a small group of followers, he opened BAANA as a private nonprofit clinic, located at 245 West 139th. A street once known as Strivers Row, it consisted of old brownstones where the cream of Harlem society formerly lived. (The four-story brownstone that was home to BAANA had been purchased from the widow of a Harlem doctor for $65,000 in August, 1979.)

Sometime in the early eighties, BAANA needed a physician, and Judy Clark's personal doctor, Alan Berkman, was chosen. His wife, Dr. Barbara Zeller, was an acupuncture student of Shakur's when her former husband joined the clinic. Later jailed for refusing to cooperate with the Federal Brink's probe, Berkman is a fugitive, having jumped bail when released. (Shakur, a fugitive since Brink's and the mastermind of the aborted robbery, is, of course, the one the law officials would most like to capture.)

A second FBI informant is a thirty-two-year-old acupuncturist who also came to BAANA from Lincoln Detox and who, under the name of Bayete, served as communications officer as well as an acupuncturist, according to Federal agents.

Lincoln Detox was not the only politically active group inspired by the Black Panthers and other Third World street youths. The roots of the Black Liberation Army (BLA), with whom the members of Lincoln Detox came to work, also sprang from the Black Panthers. That the Black Panther Party is the common root of several Brink's-related groups makes sense, since at the beginning of their history in the late sixties, the Panthers saw themselves as a group formed to fight police brutality.

Although both the Panthers and the BLA were concerned with self-defense, with the Panthers it seemed like bravado and posturing. Not so with the BLA; the BLA was serious. Instead of going after media attention, as did the Panthers, the BLA kept a clandestine profile, hoping to establish a grass-roots movement of economic and political ties with Africa. The BLA, however, did not wish to lose touch with American technology but merely to shift its economic dependency away from America. To help achieve this aim, the BLA hoped to establish self-sufficient "collectives" on the East Coast of the United States and ultimately take control of five southern states to be called New Afrika. In order to do this, the BLA needed money. But how would they get it?

It was decided that the collectives would rob rich American institutions, banks and the like, then use the money for Third World peoples. This was known as "expropriation of funds." Of course, it was also necessary for members of the BLA to support themselves. That meant establishing houses where they could reside and where they could hide the weapons necessary for "expropriations." Also, they needed cash to buy guns. However, there was a problem with the logistics of expropriation. Pulling off million-dollar robberies required planning. Lots. There was a need to train people to use weapons, as well as a need to have the money to buy them and a safe place to hide them.

But blacks, especially those with heavy criminal records, do not have an easy time obtaining credit cards, and they figured they could use some help from their white friends. Besides, blacks, in general, tend to arouse suspicion in car rental outfits, getaway cars, or at shopping malls doing pre-heist surveillance. Now, enter May 19th; what better group to take care of these matters than white women from well-to-do backgrounds with easy access to credit as well as family money, who in no way looked like criminals. It was a perfect match: the white women of the May 19th Coalition were looking for a group of black men who were serious about revolution, not college kids in it for high adventure, but "street brothers" who had already proven they were not afraid to use guns. The soldiers of the BLA fit both the psychological and strategic needs of the May 19th women.

And so was born an alliance, a curious one on the surface, despite the underlying logic. As radical lesbian feminists, the women must have felt awkward assuming subordinate positions to black macho men. How did Silvia Baraldini, one of the founders of the group, feel getting all dressed up when she went to check out the Nanuet Mall right before the Brink's robbery?

Perhaps the collaboration worked because the women had already separated themselves from men sexually. If the "brother" is no longer pressing his "foreskin privilege" upon her, it may not be awkward to use her "white skin privilege" to help him out.

Judy Clark did not seem to feel any awkwardness. A small woman, Clark, thirty-three, became the spokesperson for the May 19th group in 1978. From its headquarters in a downtown Brooklyn tenement, Clark worked with the Black Revolutionary Nationalist Movement in America, an organization that demonstrates for self-determination of blacks and against United States imperialism.

Clark, like Boudin, credits blacks with her coming of age politically. In 1980 Clark gave birth to a daughter, conceived by artificial insemination, named Harriet, presumably after Harriet Tubman. (Joanne Chesimard, the "soul" of the BLA, is also known as Harriet or Harry.)

When asked about the separation from her child while she was in prison and any possible adverse effects, Clark said she was confident her daughter would not suffer since she was being cared for by political comrades. "I don't want my child to grow up in a corrupt society," she told an interviewer for *The New York Times*. And in the newsletter, "New Afrikan Freedom Fighter," Clark said in its November 1982 special issue: ". . . For the last eleven months, I have refused to collaborate with this court's/D.A.'s/FBI's attempts to criminalize us and wage its offensive against the Black liberation struggle and anti-imperialist movement. I will never give anything of myself to you and I will continue to struggle as a freedom fighter.

"Today, you have the power to impose this mockery [the Brink's pretrial hearings]. But tomorrow, our children and even some of yours will dance on the ashes of this blood-soaked empire."

Over the past five years, the Brink's group allegedly committed eleven holdups similar to the one in Nyack, although they were not always successful. The group is also responsible for the escape of Joanne Chesimard and the kidnapping of a prison guard and matron during that escape. Nearly one million dollars in stolen money has never been recovered.

The group, which numbers at least nineteen, has threatened to kill two of its former members who have spoken with the FBI: Samuel Brown, who is awaiting trial in Rockland with Kathy, and Yvonne Thomas, the girlfriend of Sam Smith, the only Brink's suspect killed in a Queens shootout with police two days after Brink's. Smith, along with Weems, Burns, Shakur, and Tyrone "Little Brother" Rison made up the "Action Five," an elite group that ran the Brink's gang. Rison has become a chief informant for the Federal Brink's trial.

Kathy Boudin's life did not consist only of political meetings where armed robberies were planned. In what could be described as a double life, Kathy was active as a mother, participating in her son's nursery school and in other homey activities that were at the center of the lives of the small group with whom she associated. When not directly involved with the care of her child or her roommate's children, Kathy took on odd jobs, working as a waitress or serving fast foods to fans at the U.S. Open Tennis Tournament in Flushing Meadow, Queens.

Because her roommate, Rita Jensen, who worked in Stamford, Connecticut, for the town's paper, *The Advocate* could not put in the required time in her children's cooperatively run school, Kathy often substituted. The Children's Free School is located in the shadow of Columbia University and a pleasant stroll from the Boudin/Jensen sunny co-op apartment overlooking a park.

Although Kathy chose not to live with David Gilbert, the thirty-eight-year-old father of her child, she seems to have enjoyed a good relationship with him.

Gilbert, who had been active in Columbia's SDS in the mid-sixties, was also living in the area, although he was not as close to the University as Kathy. Under the alias of Lou Grossman, he rented a room in the apartment of an elderly man in the section of Manhattan known as Washington Heights, a once solidly middle-class area that until recently had a large population of older people and minorities. Gilbert paid $109 a month for the room and decorated it with posters demanding equal rights for blacks.

Lou Grossman was Lou Wasser at the moving company where he worked. On his job application he stated he had formerly been employed as a warehouseman for Itkin Brothers office furniture and as a stock clerk for B. Dalton Booksellers. Nobody at the moving company checked the application; there was no need to wonder why so sensitive and intelligent a young man would be in what many would consider an unsuitable job, for Gilbert had stated he was a writer and was working at a menial job until he finally could "make it." It was the story of most young artists.

Co-workers noted Gilbert did not have much money; he brought brown bags of health food for lunch and was often short a few dollars for the rent money.

Although his co-workers never were invited to the apartment, Kathy and Chesa, Gilbert's son, were frequent visitors, Kathy using the name of Lynn Adams in the apartment. At the Free School, she was also known as Lynn, although to the Welfare Department she was Lydia, and at the time of her arrest in Nyack she used the name Barbara Edson. When working for the tennis tournament snack concession, she told her employer her name was Elizabeth Hartwell and that she lived at the Hotel Empire across from Lincoln Center.

In order to obtain a clear picture of Gilbert's occupation before Nyack, it is necessary to go back to 1979. In December of that year, a woman who lived on Riverside Drive purchased some clothes for her young son at a shop called Broadway Baby, located near Eightieth Street. At the time, it was managed by Bernardine Dohrn. The woman paid for the clothes by check, using a driver's license for identification. The next day the Motor Vehicles Department received a request for a driver's license from a woman who said she had lost her original one. Using the name, address, and other information provided by the shopper, the applicant was granted a duplicate license.

That same day, another imposter used the name of a doctor's wife from Yonkers, who had also shopped at Broadway Baby, to obtain a driver's license that was then used to rent a van on Long Island, which later turned up in a failed, armored car holdup in Westchester. Meanwhile, the license obtained by information from the Riverside Drive shopper was used to rent a van in White Plains, which later showed up in an armored car robbery on Long Island, this time a successful one, where the robbers made off with half a million dollars. In both instances, the woman renting the vehicles used in the robberies said she was a waitress at the Blarney Castle. Then came three other rentals followed by armed robbery, all similar except the person with the fraudulent license was a man.

The police got to work investigating the last of the robberies, since in that one a guard was gunned down. In the course of their investigation, they found the Broadway Baby coincidence.

Descriptions of the renters of cars used in the holdups were issued to three hundred car rental locations in the New York area. One turned out to be a small National Car Rental agency in a black section of Brooklyn. Then on October 20, a woman came in wanting to rent a red Chevrolet van. The agency had no reason to be suspicious; she had rented from there a week before under the name of Judith Schneider. Seven hours after she left the agency, the red van showed up at the Nanuet Mall.

After the shootout, police found fingerprints on the application used in the June robbery where the guard was killed. The fingerprints turned out to be those of David Gilbert, who, authorities say, was the man who rented the cars for the other robberies, although under different names. What's more, experts concluded that the handwriting was the same as that used on a counterfeit license used to rent the van that was involved in the Chesimard escape on November 2, 1979. According to police, a copy of the car rental agreement issued in Brooklyn one week prior to Brink's was found in the apartment of Kathy Boudin.

That Broadway Baby turned out to provide police with the missing link in the string of six armed robberies makes it a suitable metaphor for the double life Kathy had pursued throughout the seventies and the dialectical dance of a psyche shuttling back and forth between guns and motherhood.

113

# LEONARD'S ATTEMPTS TO HELP HIS DAUGHTER

"I tried to stay away from active involvement. I was advised not to get close to it. But I've found it impossible to do so. I'm too close to my daughter," Leonard told *The Journal-News'* John Castelluci. Referring to Kathy's isolation, Leonard called conditions in the Rockland County Jail "inhumane." "I'm not saying that my daughter's had a nervous breakdown. I'm just saying it's taken a psychological toll."

Responding to the portrait of Kathy painted by Leonard, Rockland Sheriff Goldrick said, "He may be much more aware of that as a father. We don't see it. We see someone who appears to be very strong-willed and is taking her confinement normally."

However "normally" Kathy was taking her confinement, the intense security around the jail remained. Goldrick insisted it was necessary; Leonard disagreed: "Kathy is not going to break out of jail. The amount of work that we've done in this case indicates that we are going to use the judicial system on her behalf."

On a Wednesday afternoon late in November, Leonard arrived at the Appellate Division of the State Supreme Court, located in Brooklyn, a comfortable distance from Rockland County. Five judges were seated in high-backed chairs. After listening to Attorney Weinglass speak, Leonard stood up to address the judges himself. An impeccable dresser, Leonard looked more at ease in the stately old courtroom than he had in the less formal Rockland setting.

In a tone that neither condescended nor cowered in front of the law, Leonard pointed out that Rockland was a relatively small community and that the events were experienced as one might experience the invasion of one's own home.

Because of the intense media coverage, his daughter, he said, probably would bear the brunt of community outrage over the armored truck robbery at the Nanuet Mall and the "three terrible deaths" of a Brink's guard and two Nyack police officers. Then, standing upright as if he were a tall man who did not have to contend with a pacemaker, Leonard made his last effort to persuade them to grant a change of venue. "This," he said, looking straight at the five judges, "has become the Boudin case."

Indeed. But how had that happened? What had Leonard done to transform the Brink's case into the Boudin case?

After receiving the news that Kathy had been arrested at Nyack and telephoning his old friend and colleague, Bill Kunstler, to ask him to rush up to Nyack and act as his daughter's temporary attorney, Leonard set about choosing the attorneys who would represent Kathy officially. There was hardly a lawyer who would not have been flattered to be chosen by Leonard. The honor fell to Martin Garbus, an attorney known for fine skills at lawyering, not courtroom histrionics. With time, a second attorney, Leonard Weinglass, was chosen. He had been second in command of the defense team at the Chicago Seven trial where Kunstler had presided.

Once the business of selecting lawyers was over, Leonard began rounding up his friends on the left. Kathy had been moved out of the Rockland County Jail to the higher security

Metropolitan Correction Center in downtown Manhattan, right behind the courthouses and a short walk from Chinatown and Little Italy, where men with briefcases, judges and lawyers, could be seen taking their lunch. Kathy could see nothing from her tiny cell.

Leonard had two immediate goals: to get her out of solitary and to devise a strategy that would prove his daughter could not get a fair trial in Rockland County. Although Kathy did not like jail conditions in Manhattan, Leonard knew she would stand a better chance of an acquittal if she were tried in the city rather than in Rockland.

To make life a bit more pleasant, Leonard ordered two subscriptions for Kathy: one to *The New York Times* and the other to a less well-known publication *The Black Scholar.* If Kathy received the November-December 1981 issue, she had the chance to read about Joanne Chesimard's life behind bars in a long article called "Women In Prison: How We Are," reprinted from an April 1978 issue before she had escaped.

Benjamin Spock, a family friend and one-time client whom Leonard had successfully defended, was contacted to give his opinions on the lack of physical contact between Kathy and her young son. Relying on his authority as a pediatrician, Spock spoke out against the inhumane policy that Kathy could see, but not touch, her child.

In the meantime, Leonard's office got busy; one of his partners sent out a package to members of the Left community, soliciting support on Kathy's behalf. Included were Kathy's prison account and a lengthy legal brief citing precedents for the motion to get Kathy out of solitary. Also was the name and address of prison officials to whom recipients were asked to write.

Then Leonard remembered the time his old friend Jay Schulman, a former City College professor of sociology who was denied tenure because of his political beliefs, suggested that he be allowed to help Leonard with his Harrisburg defense. Jay had proposed using his sociological skills to survey the community and find out what kind of jurors would be most likely to side with the defense.

At first, Leonard was opposed. I imagine he would view it as faintly distasteful to use market research techniques to select a jury. After all, a jury wasn't a detergent, and even if it were, Leonard had never needed such help before. Schulman pointed out that a survey he had conducted showed that the people in Harrisburg would not be biased against Catholic priests and nuns who had committed acts of social protest. Leonard was impressed; prior to the research, he, along with the other defense attorneys, had assumed the opposite. Jay had made his point. Jury research is a valuable tool in help-ing lawyers win their cases. Jay completed the survey and Leonard won the case, making the Harrisburg Seven Trial the first for which a jury had been surveyed by professionals.

Shortly afterward, others sought such surveys. However, few lawyers had access to them and those who did had to pay fees ranging from $20,000 to $500,000. Clients like Larry Flynt of *Hustler* magazine and Claus Von Bulow whose guilty convictions are being appealed by well-known Leftist lawyer Alan Dershowitz, were not put off by such figures. In fact, along with some giant corporations, Von Bulow and Flynt are among the privileged few who can afford them.

When Jay concluded his new survey, the defense team announced there was no way Kathy could get a fair trial in Rockland County and requested a change of venue.

By now the defense had succeeded in getting Kathy out of solitary and transferred to Woodbourne Correctional Facil-ity in upstate New York. But, the defense argued, this move was not carried out in accordance with the law. In addition, the defense declared that Kathy was now isolated from the rest of the prison population.

The prosecuting attorney, asked by the defense, "Do you

have any knowledge of any other person, other than Miss Boudin, who has ever been placed in an institution for convicted people where she herself was a pre-trial detainee?" had to correct his "no" answer. "I am sorry," he said. "I guess my answers are wrong. Isn't her codefendant Judith Clark up there?" The defense was forced to concede the point. Garbus wrote: "Ms. Boudin and Ms. Clark will, alone, be together." But the defense continued to argue that "Ms. Boudin is now being held under the same conditions as her solitary confinement at Metropolitan Correction Center." Yet District Attorney Gribitz's description of her living conditions suggest a different story.

> Indeed, a cell in their unit has even been converted into a dayroom. They both [Clark and Boudin] may receive visitors in a contact setting seven days a week between the hours of 9:00 A.M. and 2:30 P.M., and, in almost every instance in which a request has been made to extend a visit in view of the distance travelled by the visitor, permission has been granted. [Contact visitation includes visits with the minor children of both women, a privilege denied other inmates at the institution.] Petitioner has full access to legal materials and to the prison commissary.

Despite long briefs arguing that Kathy was isolated, she nevertheless was able to receive a series of visitors. Leonard's office had arranged for his friends of the pacifist Left, many of whom he had defended in the past, to make the trip to Woodbourne Correctional Facility.

Two well-known Cambridge intellectuals and friends of the Boudins went to visit Kathy. One said the slayings "were unintended consequences," adding, "It should be noted that the history of the Weather Underground doesn't include a history of killing people." (Tell that to the families of Diana Oughton, Ted Gold, and Terry Robbins.)

The other, with an equally long history of political activ-

119

ism and academic stardom had this to say, "I think I can comprehend the reasons for the Brink's robbery. They're based on assumptions I don't share." Then his colleague took up the ball. "There's a struggle being waged. No question about that. The U.S. government is putting down Third World movements and using the most brutal methods." I agree. But what about the brutality of the methods used by the Brink's robbers? Even when Waverly, ironically a "Third World person" himself (although I've never heard the term used for the victims) was gunned down and spouting blood, they did not stop shooting.

Dr. Benjamin Spock described Kathy this way: "She's a person who's very identified with the poor and their problems." Tell that to the wife and children of the slain men who, while not poor, are not rich or privileged either. Or to Mary La Porta, who works hard for her money. I do not know the families of the other slain men, but I suspect that few live off income from investments and welfare checks as did many of the radicals involved. And what kind of message is this to the reactionary forces today? Just the kind they want, I would guess. See, it's rich white kids with family money and fancy co-ops who collect welfare, when not robbing banks.

But perhaps the most incredible statement comes from a radical, black folk singer/reverend who serenaded Kathy while she waited in jail. According to him, "There is no way in the world that they can kill the influence of this beautiful sister. The more they abuse her, the bigger she'll grow in the minds of young people in the movement."

I wish the minister could talk to Mary La Porta, after he sings to Kathy "Everybody's Got a Right to Live." That's the one line he and Mary could agree on.

Even Pete Seeger, a long-time friend of Jean's, got into the act. Jean called to see if he would sing for a benefit for B. J. Kids, Kathy's son's nursery school, where Bill Ayers teaches.

Seeger agreed. There is nothing wrong, I suppose, about singing to benefit innocent children, although they are hardly lacking in family resources. But aside from the indirect apology this makes for the Brink's suspects, it becomes something other than an act of kindness for his old friend, when I think of how outraged the defense team was when the Rockland paper ran an article about the fund for the children of the dead officers. Then the soliciting of Pete Seeger's talents for the benefit of Kathy's child becomes reprehensible for its hypocrisy. And that—hypocrisy—is the key word. The best example to date: a Berrigan brother coaching Kathy on how to talk effectively in court. After all, the Berrigans established their reputation by being pacifists.

I was invited to Harrisburg when the Berrigans were on trial. The Harrisburg Seven, the trial was called. A case with national prominence. Leonard was a god. But the women of the town with whom I met in health workshops had never heard of him, or anyone else connected with the case for that matter. When I explained what it was about, they were confused. If the Berrigans believed they were doing something right when they broke the law, why did they give themselves up? Only the guilty turn themselves in when they do not have to.

Shortly after, I ran into a long-time political acquaintance and friend of the Boudins. She had just come from a visit to Woodbourne. I asked our mutual friend how Kathy was. "The funny thing is, she's never looked better in her life. But I think she's desperate," was her report. The friend then said she was not part of the "briefings." Unlike one of the Berrigan Brothers, whom she said advised Kathy to give as much detail as possible at her trial, the friend was there as just that—a friend. Then she revealed that Kathy was now having serious regrets. She had told one of the Berrigans it was easy for them to advise her on how to conduct herself in court

121

because they believed in what they had done; she didn't. Not any longer. This new feeling of remorse was isolating her from the others, "freedom fighters" as their supporters called them. The friend also said that Jean seemed to be holding up even better than Leonard; she was now the strong one. But the most impressive thing was how they both were devoting everything to saving Kathy. Even the Boudin's son had been up to see his sister on several occasions.

What began to emerge was a story of a family reunion. Finally, after a decade of separation from Kathy and estrangment from the son, the family was together again. The Boudins were seeing more of Kathy now than they had since she'd left for college.

Before leaving, our mutual friend urged me to visit Kathy. Although I was excited about the prospect of seeing her, I still had some doubts. I did not want to be prejudiced so early. By going, I could be inadvertently taking part in something I did not approve of: the campaign to isolate Kathy as a special case. I felt for her predicament. As an intelligent and energetic woman, Kathy must have felt miserable in prison. Also, the separation from her young child was painful, I was certain. But what she had done was wrong; she had been part of an act—what part exactly was still unknown—that had left three people dead. It seemed as if everyone the Boudins were contacting had overlooked that, as if the deaths were an unfortunate accident. Or that Kathy's presence at the shootout was an accident.

Our friend had spoken of Kathy as living in a time capsule, being totally out of touch with reality. Even her language, she said, was confusing. It took her a while to realize when Kathy said "Euro-Americans" she meant white people.

Then, once again, she urged me to visit Kathy.

We made a date to meet before I contacted Kathy. The day before our appointment she called. She sounded uncomfortable and apologetic. She had just returned from a visit with

122

Kathy and had stopped by the Boudins. She had told them about our proposed meeting, and they had objected. Their response to a visit between Kathy and me was simple: they would try to stop it. I did not argue. I could understand their position, in a way. People don't like to be written about, and under the circumstances it made sense for the Boudins to be nervous. She said she would try to tell them how foolish they were being. Then she advised me to contact Kathy on my own.

On April 23, 1982, I wrote Kathy a letter, and on April 29 Kathy answered me with a two-page letter handwritten on a legal pad. It was a curious response. She said she was not ready to meet but sent a prison form for me to fill out that would authorize a meeting. She indicated that she was writing to me, yet she feared anything she said might be used against her.

Although I'm no handwriting expert, I couldn't help but be struck by the small uncertain script, right down to the unsuccessful attempts to cross out parts. Even more revealing was the way the pages looked: the margins got larger and the sentences smaller, so that by the second page of the legal paper, the writing formed a jagged V, corresponding to the withering away of the early strong and somewhat accusatory tone. (She had stated that writing a book about her without her permission was exploitative, something I didn't entirely disagree with.) In both content and form, the letter suggested a wary warming-up to outside contact and a disintegration of original intent. (She was writing *against* her instincts and asked that I immediately destroy the letter.) The overall impression left can be summed up by a single word: schizoid.

Kathy said she was not ruling out a meeting in the future. For the present, she did not feel in a position to meet. She did wish to correct two errors. I had written "Dear Katherine Boudin." I did not want to assume any false familiarity;

although I knew her family, it did not mean I knew her. People on the Left had criticized me for not using the formal name of an Hispanic woman, Rosaura Jimenez, in a previous book, although all the friends and family of the dead woman told me she wanted to be known as Rosie. (Leftists are good at upholding the dignity of ethnicity for others.)

Kathy seemed surprised that I did not know she was never called Katherine. (The Rockland papers and *The New York Times* referred to her that way.) She asked that in future correspondence and in my book I refer to her properly.

She said she was also dismayed at the "confusion" of origin of her son's name. Most media accounts had assumed that Chesa was named after Joanne Chesimard. This assumption is not a wild one. It was politically "correct." Anita and Abbie Hoffman named their son America (although Anita has subsequently given him a choice between that and a more conventional name; he chose the latter). A radical physician and single mother named hers Hampton, after the Chicago Black Panther shot by police. And Judy Clark's daughter is named Harriet. Chesimard was known as Harry; Harriet Tubman was a code name. And Bernardine Dohrn and Bill Ayers, who are taking care of Kathy's child, have named their children Zyad, after Zyad Shakur, a BLA member killed in a shootout with police, and Malik, after Malcolm X. Kathy herself dedicated a poem to Chesimard. Yet, without ever mentioning Chesimard, Kathy said her son had come out of the womb and into the world as if he were dancing. She called a travel agency for Kenya and asked the term in Swahili for dancing feet. They gave her a number of words, but with the help of a dictionary and a friend, the name ended up being Chesa. She said the "a" is pronounced as in "bay" or "say."

I cannot state for a fact that this is not how Chesa came to have his name. But it certainly wasn't convincing. If Kathy had been anxious at the time of his birth (as well as at the

124

time of her upcoming trial) to dispel all associations with a woman fugitive wanted for killing a state trooper, then why didn't she reject the word when the people at the travel agency gave it to her? There must be other politically compatible dialects that have a phrase for "dancing feet."

I wrote back to Kathy, thanking her for the corrections and telling her that if she had any others she would like to make, she should feel free to contact me. I did not hear from her again, although her father's secretary called me in July of 1982 to inquire if I was interested in a visit. I told her I was if Kathy was. That was the extent of our communication.

While Leonard was mobilizing the forces of the pacifist Left and visitors were streaming into Kathy's cell, petitions being filed, letters being sent, and surveys being conducted, what was Sam Brown, one of Kathy's codefendants, doing? In a word, nothing. The driver of the Honda that crashed in the heart of Nyack was sitting alone in his cell. Sam Brown, the poor black "street brother" who had already spent fifteen years behind bars, became the forgotten man, as Kathy Boudin, daughter of Leonard, stole the limelight.

As Kathy's lawyers fussed about her right to have a salad with her meals and other prison amenities, Sam Brown was beaten with wooden instruments, kicked, stomped, punched in the face and stomach, and fed heavy doses of medication. But his lawyers were not up in arms for one simple reason: Sam Brown had no lawyers. For four months, from the time of his arrest to mid-February, Brown was without *any* permanent legal counsel. On January 7, 1982, Sam Brown broke a fluorescent light fixture in his cell and used the fragments to cut his wrists. But even his suicide attempt was not considered worthy of mention, and while Kathy's lawyers continued to campaign on her behalf, Sam remained alone and forgotten.

Then suddenly Brown went from being invisible to the

front pages. "The Singing Canary," cried out the banner headlines, as stories began to appear about meetings Brown was having with agents from the FBI. And now Sam gained other important identities: to the media, he was "The Singing Canary," but to the FBI Brown was known as CSI, code for Confidential Source One.

Sam Brown was now becoming more than front-page news. He was becoming the heart of two crucial battles: the first, pitting prosecution against prosecution; and the second, prosecution against defense. How did the formerly invisible man accomplish this?

Sam Brown, Clark, Gilbert, and Boudin had all been arrested in Nyack and, hence, were prisoners of Rockland County to be tried under the laws of New York State. Although all but Brown had long histories of political ties to radical organizations, Rockland District Attorney Gribetz did not plan to bring politics into the trial; the defendants would be treated as anyone else accused of armed robbery and murder.

However, the Federal Government saw the Brink's case as an opportunity to investigate political terrorist organizations. To them, information about the network of radicals in this country was the first priority. And Brown, who was desperate to avoid spending the rest of his life in jail, was a useful man with whom to bargain. It was simple: Brown's information in exchange for his freedom.

Simple to the feds, perhaps, but not to the state. For D.A. Gribetz had no intention of letting off the man accused of pulling the trigger, even if he was willing to give information about everyone, including his codefendant Boudin.

For a long time the feds and the state fought over who "owned" Brown. After being shuttled back and forth between prisons and enduring death threats from members of the Brink's group, a compromise was reached. The Federal

Government would keep Brown for a period of time, including the start of the Federal trial, and then return him to the state in time for his participation in the trial of the Rockland defendants.

We object, cried Boudin's defense team. Brown, they pointed out, had, until the time of his voluntary cooperation with the feds, been privy to legal strategy meetings for the upcoming trial. How could Kathy's rights be protected if one of her codefendants was now working with the prosecution?

Gribetz claimed that Brown's *Federal* testimony would not in any way affect the state case; he would not allow any of it to be used. Nor would he permit a deal that got Brown off the hook.

But Kathy's lawyers knew that even if such technicalities were observed, Brown's testimony could be harmful. Already, they had evidence to upset them. First, Brown's written testimony had resulted in several police raids, and the addresses Brown supplied turned out to be accurate. That is, the police found new people the Federal authorities now knew were also involved in Brink's, although they had eluded arrest. Some had direct involvements, others indirect; all, however, were where Brown said they were, and that made Brown look reliable, at least to the FBI.

To the defense lawyers, Brown looked like a fink. Leonard, a seasoned chess player who could boast a triumph over Ché, had described Brown as a fairly decent player. But now Brown had pulled a move as tricky as a surprise checkmate. And the entire defense team would have to work on a new strategy to offset Brown's. For now, two versions of Kathy's role existed, and Brown's was quite a contrast to that of the defense. For according to the FBI, CSI had told them:

After the meeting in the Bronx, various participants, including Edward Lawrence Joseph, drove to an apartment in

127

Mount Vernon, New York, where they met Samuel Smith, Katherine Boudin, Judith Clark and others and had a second meeting. . . . During that meeting CSI said there were discussions with respect to a robbery later that day and weapons to be used in the robbery were prepared by the participants in the meeting.

Brown was posing quite a dilemma indeed. For a short time before his meeting, the defense, in an effort to secure Kathy's transfer out of Woodbourne Correctional Facility, had written up its account of "Ms. Boudin's alleged crime, her involvements and alleged background."

The indictment charges her individually and in concert with others of committing certain crimes. The only claim against her is that she was stopped while a passenger in a U-Haul. The U-Haul was not at the scene of the robbery. No one claims Kathie Boudin was at the Brink's scene. . . . If she were not the celebrated Kathie Boudin she would have been charged, as was Eve Rosahn, a former co-defendant (who allegedly supplied vehicles to some of the defendants), with criminal facilitation. *She would not even be in jail today* for she would have met, as did Eve Rosahn, the minimal bail set on her.

In light of the testimony given the FBI by Brown, the defense's argument that Kathy was in jail solely because of her celebrityhood was hard to sustain. But by pushing such an argument, the defense was reinforcing Leonard's claim that Brink's had come to mean "Boudin."

In late spring, there was a preview of things to come. A court appointed meeting was to take place among all the defendants and their lawyers. It was the first time all the suspects were to be reunited. The day of the meeting started at three in the morning when Kathy, Judy Clark, and David

Gilbert were rounded up from Woodbourne. Anthony La-Borde, since dropped from the Rockland case, was in a Queens jail, waiting trial for the murder of a Queens officer (and attempted murder of a second) two days after the Nyack crime. Burns was brought from his Brooklyn jail cell. Weems was still at Rockland County jail although there were pressures to find another place for him since the jail was an old place and not up to the security it was felt he needed.

While speaking to the FBI, Brown disclosed that the Brink's robbery was code-named The Big Dance. (Someone likes to give these events a boogie beat—Chesa coming into the world with dancing feet, Judy Clark's daughter dancing on the ashes of capitalist society.) So the big question now was: How would Brown, who had just informed on the others, be received by them?

For many months the defendants had been requesting a joint meeting to work out legal strategies together. After many delays and postponements, the meeting was finally taking place. The courts decided to take advantage of having all the defendants in one place and arranged for a lineup.

While the suspects and their attorneys were meeting, guards in New City were sealing off the entire vicinity of the courthouse. All day long witnesses were being gathered for the lineup to be held that evening. Some had been flown from the South and New England. All were marched into an improvised lineup room in a judge's chambers. The witnesses all wore masks to protect their identities. The look-alikes were all assembled at about seven when the joint meeting was over. Defense attorney Lumumba came out and issued a statement about "The Freedom Fighters," as he called the suspects, announcing that they were all united in support of Brown, who, they said, had been forced into talking with the FBI.

Then the suspects themselves issued statements of unity.

When all the issuing was over, the marshals arrived to transport them to the courthouse behind the jail. They would not budge. Gribetz had to decide whether or not to move them forcibly and decided against it. He issued a statement saying that the next time he would use whatever means necessary. At about ten-thirty that evening the hooded witnesses walked out to a deserted parking lot and went home, all at the expense of the Government. So were the transfers back to the four prisons and the overtime for the guards who ringed the building day and evening.

Although Kathy had been part of the meeting, she did not take a place in the lineup. She did not have to; one of her lawyers, Martin Garbus, had requested that he receive prior notification about any lineup involving Kathy. The request was granted so she did not have to appear.

Brown, in the spirit of the-last-hired-the-first-fired, was the only Brink's defendant who had *already* been forced to be part of a lineup.

The stage was now set for the fall of 1982, when pretrial hearings were to begin in New City, a few miles from Nyack. With LaBorde out of the State case and charged on the Federal level, the number of Rockland defendants in custody was six. On September 13, a mild sunny Monday, pretrial hearings opened in the courthouse of New City, a few miles from the shoot-out. The main street was impossible to get through, the security precautions were enormous, so were the crowds demonstrating on both sides. Those in support of "The Freedom Fighters" carried flags and yelled out "free the land," while local residents honked horns and waved American flags. New City might as well have played host to Barnum and Bailey.

Members of the media who tried to get inside the courthouse had to go through several searches, be checked with metal detectors, and had to show two sets of badges at two different checkpoints.

For those who waited the four hours to get upstairs into the courtroom, there was a different kind of circus going on. Defendants who usually stand when the judge enters, did not; instead, they, too, shouted slogans about freeing the land, claiming they were political prisoners and should be tried in front of a world tribunal.

Slowly, the TV crews packed up their equipment; by the end of the week the papers reduced the number of reporters sent to cover the hearings; defense lawyer Chokwe Lumumba flew back to Detroit and defense lawyer Susan Tipograph went home, since by now their clients were taking turns in the jailhouse yard, playing basketball. (Gilbert, Clark, Weems, and Burns had decided not to take part in the pretrial proceedings, claiming they were political prisoners, not criminals.) With these four out of the courtroom, only two defendants remained; in a shorthand version of the original alliance forged between the BLA and the May 19th Coalition, there sat Kathy Boudin, a rich, well-educated white woman, surrounded by lawyers, including a prominent father, and a poor uneducated black man, "street brother" Samuel Brown.

With the courthouse quiet again and the remaining lawyers showing respect for legal protocol, the pretrial hearings began in earnest.

The prosecution called upon a series of eyewitnesses. All had the same story to tell: Kathy Boudin was the woman they saw emerging from the passenger seat of the U-Haul; she looked scared and was yelling to the officer to put away his shotgun. Once he did, the back of the truck opened up and several black men, Samuel Brown among them, jumped out and started shooting. Kathy tried to run across the State Thruway but was caught by an off-duty correction officer who happened to be passing in his van.

The witnesses included the woman who had seen the transfer of cars behind the empty Korvettes, the two officers who had survived the shoot-out, the off-duty correction

131

officer, and a woman who was right at the shoot-out with her elderly mother when her car, waiting for a light to change, was commandeered. All but the woman in the house behind Korvettes were able to identify Kathy Boudin as the woman at the shoot-out, either leaving the U-Haul, or running across the road, or both.

The testimony was graphic; Waverly's body bobbing about as a gunman, identified as Samuel Brown, pumped additional bullets into him at close range. Kathy crying "I didn't shoot; he did," over and over again.

Kathy now sat quietly following the proceedings, except for the one time she spoke on her own behalf to say her food had been drugged the first night in jail, using as evidence that she was sleepy soon after eating. Few seemed impressed; in fact, things were looking grim, and the defense began to fight back. First, they argued, the police had no right to stop the U-Haul. They did not know its license plate, its size, or anything that would distinguish it from any other. All they had was a call from a woman saying she had seen a U-Haul with money and guns and people in masks piling into it behind an empty store.

The officer who stopped the U-Haul conceded that he would have stopped any, based on the radio broadcast, although there were no identifying details. But he added, the U-Haul appeared at the roadblock three to five minutes after the vehicle was spotted and "three to five minutes would be just about right" for the van to travel from Nanuet to Nyack.

The defense tried another tactic. The off-duty officer had no right to arrest Kathy; he had not read her her Miranda rights. Michael Koch conceded that was true, but argued that he had heard shooting, watched a cop fall, and seen Boudin run from the scene.

"For good or for bad," stated Koch, "I was going to grab her because she was fleeing the scene of a felony, an officer had been shot. If it was for good, then she would have my protection. Evidently in this case it was for bad." Koch went on to say that he did not have time to issue the Miranda warning since Boudin blurted out "I didn't shoot him. He did. I didn't shoot him," five or six times. When Koch neared Boudin, he testified that he pulled out his gun and badge and ordered her to halt. But she kept on running, and he caught her under the Mountainview overpass.

The defense did not give up. Kathy's lawyers argued that she was under police custody *before* the officers were killed, and according to law, you can't be charged with a criminal act if you are already under arrest. The prosecution said Kathy was not already under arrest, although she had been apprehended.

The defense for Boudin decided to concentrate on arguments against the witnesses most damaging to her, those who testified they saw her emerge from the U-Haul and say "Put your gun away, I'm afraid of guns." And, here, they had a powerful legal backup since the two officers at the scene who had survived the shoot-out both underwent hypnosis to help them recall any missing details within two days of the crime. The defense argued that the officers were no longer able to distinguish between their prehypnotic memory and their posthypnotic memory. Gribetz agreed not to use any of the testimony elicited after hypnosis, pointing out that there was nothing new in the latter anyway. The defense argued that the pre- and posthypnosis memory was too intermingled to make any distinction meaningful. To support their argument, they called in several experts.

Leonard pointed out that the request to move the trial was not based solely on the massive publicity and security arrangements surrounding the suspects. "It rests upon the commitment of this community [to be fair] and its involvement in this case."

Earlier, Weinglass described the high level of security and publicity and the defense surveys, which showed that passions among Rockland residents were inflamed over Brink's. He was cut off by one of the judges. "I think we all agree this case was a little out of the ordinary for Rockland," he said, pointing out that written arguments had already been submitted. What he wanted to know was why the jury selection should not at least be given a chance before anyone concluded it was hopelessly biased.

Attorneys on all sides were surprised that the Appellate Division had even agreed to consider the request to move the trial, since on June first, after being presented with all the results of the survey conducted by Jay Schulman, the Division had denied the defense's request to have the trial moved, stating it was premature and that a final decision would be made only after an attempt to select an impartial jury had proved impossible.

Weinglass continued to insist that it was impossible for Kathy to get a fair jury, although the prosecution had conducted surveys with contradictory findings.

"I found no evidence of repression of cognitive information. The substance of what they said was in essence the same before, during, and after hypnosis," said Dr. Herbert Spiegel, who has taught a graduate course on hypnosis at Columbia University's College of Physicians and Surgeons for twenty-two years.

The defense finally decided to demand that the officers who had been hypnotized submit to a psychiatric examination.

While Boudin's lawyers continued to argue that she was totally innocent, Samuel Brown stood accused of participating in every aspect of the shoot-out, starting with his presence at the mall before even a single shot was fired.

Brown was granted permission to stop attending the daily

sessions, now primarily occupied with technicalities pertaining to Boudin's defense. Kathy now sat alone, isolated from all the other defendants.

"I wish to participate but the court has made it impossible for me," she said, criticizing the presiding judge for not changing the conditions. Kathy was granted permission to stop attending the sessions. According to George Walsh, a staff writer for Rockland's *Journal-News,* "Kathy appeared progressively thinner and wearier as the hearings wore on. Her eyes were sunken and she seemed animated by anxiety as she spoke with her attorneys."

The time had arrived for drastic action. Or at least something out of the ordinary. It was time for Leonard himself to act. Of course, this wasn't the first occasion when he had acted on his daughter's behalf. As a lawyer, he had defended the group who had filmed his daughter in the movie *Underground.* And, of course, Leonard had been there with money to bail her out and to help her live. But acting on Kathy's behalf now was different. For Leonard had once stated, "I do not lose cases." (And according to the journalist who quoted him, that was the most likely reason Leonard declined to defend the Rosenbergs.) Well, this was going to be a challenge to a man with a perfect record.

The judges did not cut off Leonard Boudin nor interrupt him as they had Leonard Weinglass. They listened until Boudin was done and then said they would hand down a decision shortly. The defense arguments, of course, were not new. Once again, they made the point that Kathy's case was unique. "In no other known instance in American jurisprudence has an accused been compelled to stand trial in such a small, aroused community where the accumulated data is as massive on the issue of actual bias as that now before this court."

What was new was the evidence for such a claim that the

Shulman survey had prepared. On display were four neatly bound volumes in front of the collection boxes for the fund of the slain officers; the purple-and-black bunting that had draped Nyack's storefronts; and there were anecdotes, too. Jean, Kathy's mother, had not been able to find a single local cabdriver to take her back to the city.

Then came the 7,184 lines of local newspaper copy written about Brink's from September 13, the first day of the pretrial hearings, until November 2. The surveyors pointed out that nearly two-thirds of the pieces had appeared on the front page and almost half of them had headlines that stretched over four columns or more of print. Of course, what was not included were the articles from the same paper, *The Journal-News,* that had been used as legal exhibits, articles that had helped the defense make its points.

By stating that the Brink's case had become the Boudin case, Leonard was calling attention to another irony; were it not for the special treatment Kathy had been given, it's unlikely Brink's would have come to mean Boudin.

Yet the defense continued to single Kathy out. "Something might happen which inures to their [the four defendants not taking part in the pretrial hearings] benefit, but everything we're arguing, every move we're making is a move we'd make to defend Kathy Boudin," Leonard Weinglass said.

There was anger over the cost of the Brink's case. Estimated costs of the trial have been put at three million and that does not cover any of the 1.5 million dollars already spent by Rockland. To those already suffering the effects of a depressed economy, the new talk of a tax increase was infuriating, especially since it seemed to be going to cover the costs of keeping rich kids from going to jail. (The Boudin survey alone cost $30,000 and that was only a small fraction of the defense's costs in trying to have the trial moved.)

But something went beyond cost. The town felt it should not be accused of bias just because the men shot were well-

136

known and loved by the people. Nyack prided itself on the fairness of its residents. Again, there were startling ironies. Nyack, under normal circumstances, is the kind of place the Boudins would find sympatico.

A member of the press who has been covering Brink's for a New York City paper and who lives in the Nyack area, is married to a woman who sells real estate there. She cannot recall a single instance in which a black person has ever *not* been shown a property, even in the most exclusive areas, because of race. It was only *after* Brink's that racism arrived in the area and a man was stopped and searched by police; although innocent, he was black. And it is only *after* Brink's that the Rockland police are undergoing a totally new training, one that will prepare them to deal with armed robbers who shoot with automatic weaponry and without warning. As those who live in big cities know, this usually means that blacks will bear the burden of police "readiness." Example: not too long after Brink's, Mary La Porta was stopped by a cop in a neighboring town. Not being from the Nyack force, the cop did not recognize Mary. To him, she wasn't the exotic and sassy gal Chipper had spotted; Mary was just another nonwhite face and, like the innocent black man stopped at gunpoint right after the shoot-out, Mary too would now be subjected to the tough we-re-not-taking-any-chances post-Brink's policy adopted by the police.

The Village of Nyack lost two of its best-loved citizens precisely because it is a trusting and tolerant place. When Kathy got out and asked an officer to put his gun away, he did so. And this, despite information that a Brink's guard had just been shot, over a million dollars had just been stolen, and the armed robbers had escaped in a truck similar to the one from which she emerged. Still, the officer did not hesitate to order all guns away.

What is true is that Nyack and New City don't like the

Boudins. Not anymore. According to the press member and local resident who has been covering Brink's from the start, Leonard was particularly rude when the press asked the defense lawyers' permission to take pictures.

Kunstler and Leonard were having a sandwich in a local luncheonette when the photographer approached. Explaining that he did not wish to disturb their meal, he asked when he could take a few shots. Kunstler was obliging; Leonard was not. "I don't like the press. I don't want to cooperate with you. You can go to hell," he said. (According to the same source, Jean was extremely personable and polite, chatting with animation about her earlier years when she worked briefly for a paper.)

Yet Leonard has not always held the press in contempt; two of the journalists whose coverage of the Harrisburg Trial turned into books, themselves turned into good friends. According to the offended member of the press, such uncalled for rudeness on Leonard's part has not endeared him to the community. You don't have to spend thirty thousand dollars on a survey to learn that the Boudins might have a hard time hailing a cab in the Nyack area.

Had Kathy not been so consistently singled out, had Leonard not been so visible a part of her defense, had he not tried to argue that her incarceration was due to her fame, and had he been a bit more civil to the members of the working press, negative feelings against the Boudins would probably not have run as high as he claimed they do. And certainly, he would not have been able to argue that the Brink's case had become the Boudin case.

Venue changes are expensive and inconvenient to a community; they are also an insult. "It looks kind of defeatist and reflects rather poorly on a community for a judge to say 'we can't find an impartial jury,'" said Mark F. Pemrantz, a professor at Columbia Law School.

Perhaps one way to evaluate the fairness of a community is to take a look at it both before and after it has undergone a crime of the magnitude of Brink's.

Years before, I had spent time in Nyack with members of the Haitian community, then the second largest in the country, while researching a piece for *The New York Times* on Haitian women who had come to the States after being taught how to use a sewing machine. In Haiti there had been a national holiday to celebrate the new minimum wage of a dollar a day (since raised to $2.65 before taxes). To earn that dollar, the day started at dawn and allowed a half-hour for lunch and two five-minute breaks for the toilet. Competition for jobs was intense. When the women learned to sew in pockets and seams at close to 100 percent efficiency, they were given a piece of chewing gum. Some had heard that with the newly acquired skills, you could earn almost one hundred dollars a week in New York for the same amount of work. Most did not believe it until they learned it was true. And, if they were really industrious, they could also work as a domestic in an office building at night and come close to doubling their weekly wages.

When I interviewed women who had migrated from Haiti to Nyack, I found a sense of jubilance. I asked a woman if she had any idea what the owner of the factory made. When she shook her head, and I gave her the figure, I realized she could not comprehend it any more than I can comprehend how many stars are in the universe. The figure is beyond my experience. One of the Haitian men, a trained pharmacist who had been here longer and came from a middle class family, told me of the time he had accompanied his father to the hotel area of Port-Au-Prince. They had peered over some hedges and saw a body of water too small to be an ocean but too large for anything to do with plumbing. No one was in it, and they couldn't guess its function. It was impossible for either of them, from a small town where none of the houses had running water, to conceptualize "pool"—a body of water built into the earth merely for fun. The pharmacist said that was what it was like for the Haitians to imagine the owners of the factories earning millions of dollars a year, while they worked below the minimum wage because most were illegal aliens.

Through their children, who translated, the women spoke of the United States as a land of golden opportunity. By having three generations work in the factories (the children worked after school, and the parents usually held two jobs, while the grandparents worked in the factories, and then came home and cooked), they were able to save enough money to buy the old wooden frame houses in the heart of the Village of Nyack. In fact, Nyack at night resembles Port-au-Prince, where the houses of the rich sparkle from the hills above the harbor.

When I visited Nyack in 1975, I was surprised how easily the new immigrants fit in, how well they seemed to be accepted. There were no reports of racial incidents among this group who spoke a strange patois, a mixture of African dialect and French. They cooked in the little patches of garden outside their homes over burning charcoal much the way they had in Haiti. I was told they also practiced a combination of voodoo and Catholicism as they had in Haiti. The appearance of an idealized American hamlet was deceptive. Nyack was a small melting pot more tolerant than any American city in which I had ever lived or visited.

The thought that the dead officer might have been involved with this community interested me. That the only black officer on the twenty-two-member force was gunned down by members of the Black Liberation Army only days before thirty-three drowned Haitians were washed up on a Forida beach, their bodies reflected in the lights of the expen-

140

sive waterfront condos, was just the sort of imagery Boudin and the rest of the Weather Underground would have seized upon at another time.

In April of 1982, I decided to pay another visit to Nyack. I wanted to sense the setting of Kathy's last adventure. I also wanted to learn about the only black police officer on the Nyack force, one of the victims of the shoot-out. I had thought an article in the newspaper had mentioned he was active in the Haitian community. This interested me for several reasons. The first was an obvious irony.

The group that ambushed the police consisted of radicals from the white Underground and the Black Liberation Army. That the *only* black officer should be killed by them, in the name of liberating blacks and other oppressed groups, was almost too glib a way to point out the fallacy in their ideology. After all, to use Kathy's jargon, the black cop was no "Euro-American," but a genuine member of the "Third World."

I arrived in Nyack late Saturday afternoon with Hal Davis, a court reporter for the *New York Post* who had agreed to work with me on this story, as he had on others. We carried a large laundry bag with newspaper clippings into one of the new restaurants in the heart of the village. After determining that it was not a boutique, but a place to eat, we took in the decor of the gentrified pub and gave our orders. Then we spread out the clippings to find the black officer's name. I phoned Information for his address. He was not listed.

At twenty to five we raced to the Nyack library, the only Carnegie Library in the county. Built with the cobblestone that characterizes the Carnegie libraries, the building felt like an old hunting lodge, with its massive fireplace, fine woodwork, old lights, and portrait of Carnegie. However, the town had updated the building with a cedar deck, sliding glass doors, and microfilm-Xerox machine.

It was about to close when we asked the librarian for copies of the local newspaper, *The Journal-News,* the week of October twentieth. She was most obliging (I had told her why we needed them), and we started Xeroxing microfilm like crazy. It was hard to believe how thorough the coverage had been. Pages and pages. Pictures, too. I asked the librarian if she happened to know where the dead officer, Waverly Brown, had lived. She said that most cops don't list their address, but she thought it was not in Nyack. That eliminated my last-ditch plan of roaming 'round the village hoping to stumble upon neighbors.

Then I saw a picture of a fair-skinned woman with her hair pulled back and up, and with chiseled features. "Girlfriend of Waverly Brown." Although the lights were flickering to indicate the place was about to close, I dashed back to the librarian, asked for a local telephone directory, and looked up the address of Mary La Porta. This time we were in luck. Although there was no street number, a street followed her name. "High." We thanked the librarian, who wished us good luck, and ran to a book store for a map. They had a Hagstrom. We found High Street. It was in the heart of the Haitian community. And it was nearby. It was an unusually hot and humid day for mid-April; I suggested to Hal we stroll over and talk to people sitting out on their porches or stoops. Hal agreed, and we set off to High Street.

We stopped in a place called Liberty Crafts; it had African artifacts and I thought it a likely spot for news of the Haitian community. But the women who ran it, one black, one white, knew nothing about Mary La Porta or Waverly Brown. They told us what a tragedy the entire thing had been.

Right down the street was an auto repair shop; I saw a group of young men. I recognized the patois. I asked them about Mary La Porta, but they looked totally confused. When I asked if they knew where we could stay the night (I was determined to find out something even if it meant staying over), they didn't. Back on Broadway I approached a young officer sitting by the window of a luncheonette. He said he knew nothing, but even if he did, he would not talk. He suggested we'd have little luck with anyone in town. I started to go up to strangers at random. But no one seemed to know anything. It was hard to know if people were genuinely ignorant or just resentful of reporters inquiring about a tragedy. For one thing was clear: everyone, from the owners of boutiques to the cop on the beat, spoke of the shoot-out as a tragedy for the entire village.

Hal spotted a tropical grocery run by some black men. I walked in and took my time selecting a bottle of soda as I sized up the place. Then I went up to a man at the counter. He, too, had been talking in patois. First, I asked if he knew of a place to stay. He took out a large batch of keys and pointed to a young man who would drive us to a motel. (Our car was in a village lot.) I told him I was interested in checking out the place, and we shook hands. But first, I wanted to reach a Mary La Porta; did he by any chance know her? He asked me to repeat the name. I handed him the slip with the name and the telephone number, adding that she lived on High Street. He took the slip and grabbed a phone behind the counter. (Hal and I had already deduced that this was probably one of the first places newly arrived Haitians are sent). Before I could think through what I'd say, he handed me the phone.

"Mary La Porta?"

"Yes," she answered.

"My name is Ellen Frankfort. Uh, I'd like to talk with you, but not on the telephone. I'm wondering if we could meet."

Mary said sure and gave directions to her place. The directory, it turned out, was out of date. She did not live on High Street, not any more, but she had the same phone. I thanked the man behind the counter and told him I'd return.

Hal and I drove about a mile up a steep hill, made a right at an intersection, drove past the entrance to the New York State Thruway (we didn't notice the two wreaths placed at the edge of the ramp), and turned into a new, three-story, red-brick apartment complex spread in three layers up a wooded mountainous area from which you could glimpse all of Nyack and the Hudson Rover. We'd been so intent on getting there that neither of us had thought about what to say when we met her.

We knocked at the door; a woman opened it and told us to come in. She was about 5′ 6″ and slender. Her face was intriguing; she had the coloring of a Filipino or an American Indian. Her hair was pulled back as in the picture; it was dark with a few streaks of gray. I wasn't certain of her background or even her race, but whatever she was, she was striking, although she looked a bit tired.

Once we were in, I commented on her sense of trust. "I mean, you don't know us, you have no idea why we're here, and yet you just opened the door and let us in." She allowed that most people warned her not to be so trusting, but that was how she was. I wondered if she would feel the same way once I announced why we had come. To my delight, she seemed more trusting, more open. Of course, she would answer any questions. I began to realize that, although she was a living victim of Brink's, no one had asked her story, how she felt about the whole thing.

We spoke for about three hours; she sounded angry whenever she spoke of "them." She also asked us what we knew of the legal proceedings. Whether they would get the chair. She made it clear that she hoped they would. Hal had been sitting on the floor against the wall. (The apartment was sparsely furnished; she was selling her old furniture and had been preparing to make room for Waverly's. In fact, when we called, she thought we were coming to look at the furniture for sale, she told us at the end of the three hours.)

144

Mary and I sat facing each other; I had learned not to get right into a straight question-and-answer format if you want to learn about a person, but let her lead the way as much as possible. Mary spoke of the last day, how she found out Chipper had died. But it was when Hal chirped up from the corner, "How did you meet him?" that she became filled with emotion. "You really want to know?" We told her we did. Her response was moving. It was clear she did not think any reporter was interested in her. In all the coverage that had taken place since October 20, the media had focused on the "alleged killers." Kathy Boudin had been written up in *People Magazine,* and Mary made it clear that she did not understand why such people were being treated like stars. Mixed with the anger and hurt and the talk of the electric chair were statements that blew my mind. "Waverly was some mother's son just like this Mr. Boodeen," as she called him.

As we were about to leave, Mary brought us over to three piles of newspapers, each about two feet high. She said I could have any that would help with my work. I was overwhelmed. There were so many, and Nyack and Waverly and Mary were all spinning around in my head. Fortunately, Hal made the choices and picked out three from the week of October twentieth. I told Mary I would like to take her out to dinner, but that I was too tired. I promised to return the next day for a visit. I wanted to get back to the city and Xerox the papers before returning to Nyack.

I stayed up the entire night reading the papers. I couldn't get over how complicated the day of the shoot-out was. So many people, so many cars, so many aliases. But it was Mary who captured my interest. Just as the Boudins' residential block could be a metaphor for the life-style of the Bohemian aristocrat, Mary, too, assumed a symbolic meaning. She was a working-class black woman. She, like Kathy, seemed strong. She had declared with great pride, "I'm a union woman," and had been, it turns out, among the first blacks to be employed at Lederle, where she works as a machine operator. She had even turned down a supervisory job to stay in the union. Mary was not about to sacrifice her principles for a title.

What I found most attractive was the fact she held strong opinions. Mary was apolitical in traditional terms. She had not heard of Spock, Boudin, Kunstler, Weinglass, or any of the celebrated Leftists. In her speech, she advocated violence for those who have been violent towards others. But in practice, she was warm, trusting, and generous. She also seemed tolerant of difference. After all, Mary had lived for ten years in a small town as what many would call the "mistress." But Mary didn't think of herself that way, and it seemed clear that neither did Waverly or his family, neither his blood family, or his family of peers, the police. She spoke with a striking tolerance of gays, blacks, whites, the old, and young. When she spoke of her feelings of anger and her desire for revenge, it seemed she was being true to how she felt. But it was hard to believe that she would hurt anyone. It was as if Mary did not have secrets to hide, did not feel guilt or shame about herself or her life. It was clear that she and Waverly had worked hard; and for ten years both had enjoyed and been devoted to each other.

Mary set the record straight, with no apologies, on Waverly's relation to the Haitian community. Waverly did not relate to one group or another on the basis of color (although Mary did not word it that way). If anything, Waverly and Mary, like the Haitians, were happy with everything American, the convenient shopping centers, the TV, the newly air-conditioned apartment units.

What kind of twisted thinking could make Kathy believe that people such as Mary and Waverly, both "Third World,"

146

wanted a bloody revolution? Kathy spent time in Russia and Cuba; she met with delegations of Vietnamese. It is hard to visit any country, especially one whose people have some political awareness, and not be struck by their desire for progress, for some material comfort—flashlights and radios, batteries, TVs, cameras—no matter what the politics.

I have spent time in the Caribbean. I've been to Puerto Rico, Haiti, and Jamaica twenty-one times. Jamaica and Haiti are an interesting contrast: in the dictatorship, people are more likely to be subservient (called happy and smiling and childlike, in travel brochures) and to adopt a quasi-religious fatalism about their lot in life. In Jamaica, where I got to know some of the people who had worked with Socialist leader Michael Manley, I found things to be very different. (Also, in Puerto Rico, where I had contacts with the Independence Movement.) There was, of course, strong anti-American feeling. No one wanted to be American. Yet, if you went to any of the cities or the small mountain villages, including those where the people had never seen a white person, all would grab a one-way ticket to the States. It is a painful dilemma if you get to know the people individually; they all want you to sponsor them to the States.

How did this go unnoticed by Kathy? One thing is difficult to overlook in the lives of all the sixties underground people and their above-ground sympathizers: their endless travel around the globe.

Yet Kathy seemed unaware there could exist a place in the United States where blacks and whites are integrated. A mere stroll around Nyack might have taught her something about her native land.

Nyack has a fine book store, and it was there I purchased, for one dollar, a packet of annotated maps called *Rediscovering the Nyacks,* published by the Friends of the Nyacks, described on the cover as an "organization dedicated to con-

tinuing and improving the appealing way of life long established in the Nyacks." I also purchased a booklet called
*South Nyack Centennial 1878-1978*. It was here I learned, on
the very first page, that Nyack had been part of the underground railroad "and this along with refugees from the
potato famine in Ireland served to increase the racial mix in
the area." But what really stunned me was the description of
the Rockland Female Institute:

> As early as 1854 plans for a school in the South Nyack area
> were underway. To be called the Rockland Female Institute,
> it was to be modeled on the Mount Holyoke Seminary, the
> first institution of higher learning for women in the United
> States.

The article goes on to describe the curriculum, which included algebra, geometry, natural science, and mental science
(whatever that is), among its many courses. As the Female
Institute, it clearly gave Nyack an early start in feminism,
which I think may explain some of the appeal of the town
today.

At the turn of the century, when merchants began to
prosper and a well-to-do and enlightened population had
moved in to share the land with the Indians and the many
immigrants, the Female Institute became a military academy. Then in 1925, the military academy gave way to a social
club, called the River Club, with gazebos, wicker porch furniture, an indoor cafe, and a ballroom with rattan tables strewn
with potted plants, much in the style of the recently restored
little eateries in the heart of the village.

When I read that the club went up in flames in 1932, I
couldn't help but think of Kathy. A place that started out as a
radical place of learning for women to come to its end in a
"four-hour-long, three-alarm early morning fire" had an
uncomfortably pat metaphoric rightness.

But, in the end, it was Mary who made what happened in Nyack so starkly ludicrous as an act of political change. Mary, a black woman, fits into the community with no problems at all. While I waited for her in the small lobby of the motel, I had a chance to observe what it's like to arrive in Nyack. Poor-looking blacks, who took out rumpled bills from overalls, stood at the register next to young people with bicycles who had come to enjoy the scenic bicycle route along the river and the town's Victorian gems, or to stroll around the crafts fair scheduled for that Sunday. Perhaps having an underground railroad for many years, the first Female Institute, a continuing theater community, and an active women's political group all contributed to the impressive mood of tolerance.

In addition, Nyack was also home to a large homosexual population. This particular mix is not unique to quaint towns that have a coven of crafters and the rich history of trade of a river village. What makes it unusual is that the Nyacks and the surrounding Rockland County communities also have an unusually large proportion of police officers, a point made by the survey commissioned by the Boudin legal defense to prove that Kathy could not get a fair trial in Rockland.

It seemed the book was turning into a study in ironic ambience. After all, Leonard Boudin has established his reputation by defending the constitutional rights of political dissenters. I could understand his reluctance to talk, but to censor, in effect, another person, provided a striking contrast to Mary. Mary was angry that innocent people had been killed. She did not understand how any ideology could justify killing. To her, it was simple. Killing is wrong. But the Boudins acted as if their daughter were totally innocent. It was a ticklish situation. The entire Left, its true patriarchs, were being called upon to do what they could on behalf of Leonard and his life-long record of devotion to political dissidents.

Yet, almost all those he defended were heroes, albeit of the Left.

In contrast, Mary was not a hero. She was, however, the kind of woman I suspect Kathy would have admired.

Almost from the time I walked in, I had sensed a kindred spirit. Someone who follows her feelings and doesn't put up with crap. I was also moved at some of the details I learned, such as that Waverly's last purchase before his death was the turkeys for senior citizens.

On May 15, I made another trip to Nyack. As it turns out, that is the day set aside to commemorate all police officers killed in the line of duty throughout the country. The police halls were draped, and officers around the United States were wearing black ribbons on their badges. There was no need, however, for the Nyack Police Force to put on the ribbons; they hadn't taken them off since October 20 and planned to keep them on for one year.

Although a woman of strong convictions, Mary was not obsessed with revenge. She and I spent a pleasant evening getting to know one another. I asked her to suggest a restaurant she liked. We went to a steak joint, run cafeteria-style. When I said, "Mary, don't worry about money, this is on me." She replied, "It doesn't matter who is paying. I mean, you still want to get your money's worth." To Mary, the charming, restored little eateries were clearly not places to get your money's worth.

The visit had been so pleasant that we agreed to meet for coffee the next morning. Mary brought along a friend, Ruthie, who is white. Again, it was clear that integration was just taken for granted. What confused Ruthie and Mary was all the business about expropriating funds for the Third World. Mary and Waverly were Third World, although they would never separate themselves out. Mary felt that for people to act "as if we voted for them to represent us" when robbing banks, just showed how out of it they were. And the

150

mumbo-jumbo names that made everyone sound as if they had just stepped off the set of *Roots* was another joke. There was no need to manufacture roots; Nyack had more than anyone could ask for.

I couldn't help but feel that the architecture of the town, its sheer diversity, also allowed difference to flourish. It was the Boudins and their liberal comrades who seemed to be distinguishing between black and white, the right people and the wrong ones. In all the Leftists lined up to brief Kathy in jail, there were no radical feminists called upon, as far as I know. Why weren't Gloria Steinem, Kate Millet, Robin Morgan, Adrienne Rich invited up if, as I had been told, the point was to bring Kathy up to date with political reality?

Again, before we set off for home, Mary volunteered a stack of papers that had coverage of the Brink's proceedings. She asked if I would remember her and keep in touch. I kidded her about even asking, and then Ruthie, she, and I all embraced and said good bye. I told her I would keep in touch. And I did. Sometimes I called just to see how she was feeling; usually, she told me of some new legal development.

In July, I learned that she was sick. She had been to the hospital; they told her it was "nerves." Nerves, I thought. The woman's ailment. Like Kathy's mother, who had, in her own words, suffered from nerves; like Patty Hearst's mother, who confessed the same to Barbara Walters; like my own mother, and countless mothers of friends. What did it mean to suffer from nerves? For the older women, it seemed to mean a way to protest things that were still private, a certain emptiness and a sense of waste. This was particularly true for the women who had sacrificed their own careers and artistic talents for those of their husbands. Fortunately, Mary had always been independent, and with some rest, she was back on the job.

We spoke about the endless delays in pretrial hearings.

151

They had been postponed three times. There was a sense of letdown with each delay. I think Mary needed to know that something was happening, justice was proceeding. She had a deeply felt sense of injustice, which may have had to do with her own background. It wasn't ideological; it was humane. I could see the common theme running through all our lives as women (even that of Kathy). The theme of family ties, filial ties, seemed critically important. There was no doubt that Waverly and his family had become the one Mary had never known. And I think she focused on Kathy because Kathy, in contrast to all the other suspects, seemed to be surrounded by endless family support. And that support, as far as Mary could tell, accomplished nothing except further delay of the process of justice.

In one of our conversations over the summer, when nothing was moving legally, Mary said, "You might think this sounds stupid. Tell me if it does. But I don't. I mean if these people come from money [and by Mary's standards the Boudins do] why don't *they* pay for all the expenses?"

Mary was referring to the enormous expenses Rockland County was incurring for security. Anticipating a three million dollar tab for trial security, even if held outside Rockland, officials talked of increasing the local taxes unless the Federal Government helped out.

Throughout the spring there had been many hearings and meetings. Each time one of the defendants was moved, a convoy of police cruisers had to go along; every time one of them made a court appearance, there were extra security guards. Things were so extreme that all strangers were frisked and put through a metal detector as if boarding a plane. Guns were outside the courtroom and inside as well. Kunstler was the first to protest, arguing that the security gave the impression that the suspects were wild animals.

I do not like an atmosphere of military seige. Yet when I

read the criminal records of some of the Brink's suspects, I did not think it excessive. Several were linked to the escape of Joanne Chesimard; even one of the attorneys had suspected links with jailbreaks. (Tipograph was, according to police, involved not only in Willie Morale's escape, but also in that of Marilyn Buck, one of the two Brink's suspects still at large.)

And they weren't the ordinary sort. Some were highly fanciful, comandeering helicopters to land atop the large prison in downtown New York.

The plan police uncovered for Thanksgiving Day 1981 would have to be the winner, at least for "Mission Impossible" innovative thinking. According to the police, a group of radicals had bought an old fire engine at an auction; then they broke into a uniform supply place in Queens and took the appropriate costumes. Then someone was to call a firehouse near the Kings County Hospital prison ward where Brink's suspect Nathaniel Burns was housed after receiving wounds in a fight with police. (Almost all the male suspects have histories of struggle with police, if not actual murder.) The caller was to identify himself as a Cub Scout leader interested in taking his troop on a tour of the firehouse. According to plans seized by detectives, the so-called Boy Scoutleader was to slip into the firehouse and use its communications system to register a fake fire alarm at the hospital ward where Burns was. In the ensuing chaos, Burns would be whisked away.

But the most costly single event for Rockland before trial probably occurred the night all the defendants were to be reunited for the first time since arrest in a court-appointed meeting that would include the attorneys as well.

When such a meeting takes place, each suspect is accompanied by several cars. ("Oh, the traffic tie-ups alone," Mary said.)

Mary, of course, had a point. I did not think it stupid. (Nor

153

did the Conservative politician who proposed it to the local legislature long after Mary first brought it up.)

It made sense to have those with money pick up the tab instead of having the working class pay for what they saw as the defiant acts of a group of killers, when they were already hurting from the economy. It was, ironically, a socialistic notion. In a more just society, the rich, particularly those who had already laid out large sums for the legal process, surveys, and the like, would pay for the cost of keeping their children behind bars while they tried to delay the legal process. Mary was slowly beginning to believe that she had been wrong. The legal system did not concern itself with right or wrong; there were too many technicalities before they could deal with that. Mary was still counting on the jury at the trial, whenever that would be.

Once again the defense had succeeded in delaying things by requesting, for the second time, a change of venue. Although the request was made on behalf of Kathy only, since she was charged with acting in concert, she could not be tried separately.

Samuel Brown was the only other defendant who had joined in seeking to move the trial. However, the legal arguments presented to the judge who was to decide, were, again, made only for Kathy.

Then, shortly before the Christmas holidays and the end of the year, the judges announced their decision. Once again, Leonard could say, "I do not lose cases." For the Appellate Court had decided to grant the request for a change of venue.

But this time Leonard's victory was more illusory than real. For although the change was granted, the trial was now set to take place in nearby Orange County, a far cry from the urban locale the defense had argued for, stating that city people have more diverse views and that no single event can dominate the news as Brink's had in Rockland.

Reluctantly, the defense had to settle for a county similar to Rockland in age and racial mix, except it is less wealthy, more rural, and most important, more conservative. If it proved impossible to select a fair jury there, the defense said, it would once again request a change of venue.

In mid-June, less than one month before the scheduled start of Kathy's trial in Orange County, Leonard traveled to Utica, New York, where he and Assistant District Attorney John Edwards presented the arguments involving a second change of venue. Once again Leonard argued that intense publicity and security precautions would prejudice potential jurors. But this time Leonard could not claim a victory. The State's highest court refused to grant Kathy the right to appeal the December decision of the Appellate Division that had moved the case out of Rockland and into Orange County.

Then less than two weeks before the scheduled date of the trial, Judge David Ritter ordered Brown's case severed after the defendant's lawyer, Peter Branti, said he was placed in a position of divided loyalties since he had previously represented codefendant David Gilbert. Once again, Sam Brown was to go it alone. And as a spin-off of the decision, Rockland County was now burdened with the cost of *two* trials, neither of them in Rockland.

Within a week of the Brown decision and less than a week from the start of the State trial on July 11, 1983, another decision was handed down. New York State's highest court ruled hypnosis an unreliable means of recollection and, therefore, testimony induced by hypnosis unacceptable in court. Kathy's chief counsel, Martin Garbus was jubilant, claiming the decision a "major victory" which could "dramatically change the trial."

Almost immediately after this decision, another was handed down, and it is doubtful that Garbus was thrilled. Kathy was now going to be tried separately from Clark, Gilbert, and Weems, but not alone as the counsel had sought.

Nor was Samuel Brown going to be tried alone, after all. Together Boudin and Brown would stand trial in Orange County, with the scheduled date set for October 12, 1983, close to October 20, the second anniversary of the deaths of Paige, Chipper, and O'Grady.

Shortly before the Manhattan trial being handled by the Federal Government, there was a new revelation. The Brink's defendants had not all acted out of political passions, a wish to improve the conditions of oppressed people, as the Rockland Freedom Fighters and their sympathizers maintained. Not, at any rate, according to the latest informant, Tyrone "Little Brother" Rison.

Rison had been a member of Action Five—the group of black men, including Shakur, Burns, Weems, and Samuel Smith—who carried out the armored car robberies while the white women acted as decoys. Now, like Brown, Rison was out to save himself and his family. By agreeing to cooperate with the FBI, Rison had already secured the release of his wife who had been serving time in Georgia for robbing a local bank of $5,500. Rison had already served seven months for the same crime.

But that was petty stuff compared to other activities. Rison revealed that in addition to the armored car robberies, some Brink's defendants were heavily involved in drugs. Mutulu Shakur, the founder of Lincoln Detox, was himself a heavy user of cocaine and BAANA, the Harlem acupuncture center that served as the unofficial headquarters for the Brink's members, was a busy drug-trafficking center.

Rison said his "turning point" came on June 2, 1981. Stuck in a car with a jammed door, he was unable to stop his companions from shooting to death an armored car guard outside a bank in a Bronx shopping center. Moreover, the $250,000 taken was not "expropriations" for the "Third

156

World." Some of it, according to Rison, was going to buy drugs.

Rison revealed some more unknown facts about the Chesimard escape and other armored car robberies, including Brink's, which he had opposed, arguing the Nanuet Mall area was too well-protected.

Then Rison exploded a big bombshell: one of the Brink's defendants, a drug dealer, was operating a call-girl ring right in the midst of the ring of radical feminists.

Things were taking a foul turn, and by now it was clear that it was each man for himself and each woman for herself. Except Kathy Boudin was not exactly alone. Her defense team, having given up all pretenses at "unity," had already petitioned for a separate trial. Kathy was now going to use her "white skin privilege" on her own behalf, even if it was at the expense of codefendants Samuel Brown, and David Gilbert, the father of her own child.

Attorney Weinglass would no longer be able to talk about the "biracial" mix of the defendants, as he had when arguing for a change of venue. All that remained "biracial" now were a black and a white cop, buried within a short distance of one another.

Shortly after Kathy's arrest, Leonard, as previously noted, had a subscription of *The Black Scholar* sent to her in jail. It is in that publication I read that whites are jailed at a rate of 43.5 per hundred thousand, while black prisoners number 367.5 per hundred thousand and are sentenced, on the average, to 20 percent longer terms than whites.

It is, perhaps, the final irony that Leonard's own choice of reading matter for his daughter would turn into a scenario, of sorts, for her legal defense. An irony, but not a surprise.

Only a few months earlier, Kathy's long-time political comrade Bernardine Dohrn, the proprietor of Broadway Baby and the woman caring for Kathy's child, admitted that her access to important and well-connected lawyers was responsible for her release from prison. (She had been jailed for eight months when she refused to cooperate with officials investigating Brink's). Her black "sisters," lacking the money to hire expensive "ruling class" lawyers, were left to wait out their time behind bars.

Nor do "ruling class" lawyers hesitate to use their skills to obtain taxpayer money for reimbursement. When Martin Garbus won the lawsuit he filed against the Federal Government for placing Kathy in solitary confinement, he requested $75,480, stating he had spent 1,006 hours on this aspect of the case—a "complex and difficult" one. The judge disagreed about the complexity, and Garbus was awarded the normal fee, $75 an hour, rather than $175.

It doesn't seem complex to me either. The suit rested, in part, on Kathy's own description of prison life in solitary. You don't have to be a skilled lawyer to recognize her conditions as punitive and inhumane. Where the skill comes in is in knowing how to implement a law passed only nineteen days earlier: The Equal Access to Justice Act.

It is also worth noting that when Samuel Brown finally did get a lawyer, she had to petition for $35 an hour—the rate granted by the state for attorneys of those without any funds of their own. This is one-fifth of what Garbus had asked for.

Just as *The Black Scholar* might have predicted.

Then in June 1983, just before Kathy's pre-trial hearings were to start, more documents pertaining to a call girl ring were found in a Greenwich Village apartment used by the Brink's "family," as they call themselves.

According to papers seized, the 85 Barrow Street apartment was not a "safe house," and the money stolen was not all going to the poor and oppressed. Drugs and sex were also involved, as previously suspected. Two 22-gram bottles of mannitol, a substance used to cut coke, were found. Edward Joseph, one of the defendants in the ongoing Federal Brink's trial, is believed to have rented the apartment with a woman who is now a fugitive.

It is also believed that Mutulu Shakur, the mastermind of Brink's, hid out at Barrow for six weeks, fleeing on the day before the FBI zoomed in on Joseph and Ferguson, March 25, 1982, arrests made possible by Sam Brown's testimony.

To make matters even worse for Kathy's defense team, the same day the news broke about Tipograph's connections to the Morales escape and those between Brink's and the FALN, Judge Ritter, presiding over the state trial, ruled that Kathy could not be tried separately from the others.

June 2, the first day of Kathy's pre-trial hearings, was something of a horror show for her defense team. A wild melee broke out in the courtroom, and supporters screamed, "Free the land," and, "Judge Ritter, you can't hide, we charge you with genocide."

The judge was not the only target of ridicule and contempt. The band of demonstrators screamed "traitor" as soon as Sam Brown was brought in. The shouting escalated into a brawl between guards and demonstrators. Sam Brown was whisked out a side door, and the hearing came to a halt.

July 11, the date set for Kathy's trial, was not far away. Suddenly, after a lifetime of relative obscurity (relative, at least, to Leonard), Jean emerged as a serious poet, giving public readings and radio interviews. Jean came across as charming, poised, and articulate. She spoke at length about her new book of poetry, published by a small press with a printing of 500 and obtainable through Leonard's office, among other places.

After reading several poems and discussing Kathy's childhood, she was finally asked about Brink's. (This interview, on WNYC, the official municipal radio station, happened to take place two days before the start of Kathy's pre-trial hearings.)

"It's very painful," Jean responded. "I last saw her on her

birthday [May 19] about ten days ago, with her son. When you look at those two, you can't believe . . ." After a pause Jean resumed in a faltering voice. "She is really a very loving person, and the child Chesa is a very lovely child. When you see them embrace on the prison grounds, they're so loving."

Then Jean added, "The tragedy of this is so unbearable." And with a mixture of what sounded like sobs and sighs, she went on to say, "At least Kathy is alive," while expressing audible grief that other children had lost their fathers.

The same day as the pre-trial courtroom brawl, an interview with Jean, joined by Leonard, was aired at eleven in the evening over the classical music station of *The New York Times,* WQXR. Again, the ostensible reason was Jean's newly published book of poetry, *Some of the Parts.* Jean read a few poems but this time there was no expression, at least in the presence of Leonard, of sorrow for the children left fatherless by the Brink's shootout. And when Leonard spoke, he concentrated mainly on the police brutality in Chicago in 1968 and the current inhuman jail conditions to which his daughter was being subjected.

Whether Kathy is as lucky as Dohrn remains to be seen. Kathy is accused of felony murder. Put simply, that means that if you commit an armed robbery, you are guilty of a felony. If, during that robbery, someone dies, you are guilty of felony murder.

Kathy's alleged cry, "I didn't shoot him. He did."—even if believed by a jury—is not much help in New York State, which has a felony-murder statute. That means anyone who commits a felony in which someone dies can be convicted of murder, even if there was no intent to kill.

Now, couple that with the provision in New York State law that "acting in concert" with other felons makes you just as guilty, no matter who pulls the trigger, and it is easy to see why Kathy's defense was anxious to separate her from her codefendants.

The minimum sentence for murder in New York State is fifteen years to life in prison. The maximum term is twenty-five years to life. Not so long ago, killing a police officer in New York brought the death penalty. But not on Tuesday, October 20, 1981, the day Leonard was informed his daughter had been arrested.

The courts will determine how much longer Kathy remains imprisoned. Whatever the final verdict, there remains one question the courts cannot decide: How did Kathy Boudin, daughter of a distinguished civil rights attorney father and a pacifist/poet mother wind up on trial for thirteen counts of murder, robbery, and assault? In other words: what went wrong?

# PART THREE

# *REFLECTIONS*

# 5

# WHAT WENT WRONG?

IF Boudin's arrest marks the end of an era, the psychological unraveling of her life, from young girl to adult revolutionary, raises the most contemporary issues. Boudin at thirty-nine, a revolutionary woman who chose to live on the edge, is not so different from other women in their late thirties who choose to become mothers as their reproductive years fade. Yet her choice is puzzling: what made Kathy think she could both raise a child in health and change the world through violent revolution? How did this woman who tried to have everything wind up in the tragic straits of the desperado?

The stories of stars who end up tragically, such as Marilyn Monroe, Janis Joplin, John Belushi, Edie Sedgwick, and even those who don't end up dead, exert a magnetic pull on the imagination. Like them, Kathy Boudin is a star, a movement star of the sixties.

(Even the other members of the Brink's team were aware of her legendary status. The night of Boudin's arrest, Sam Smith, who got away only to be killed two days later in a Queens shootout, commented on what a bombshell it would be when Barbara Edson's real identity was learned.)

In fact, the story of Kathy Boudin is the story of the stars of the intellectual Left.

As 1980 dawned and the networks cranked out their

165

reviews of the decade, it became the journalists' task to state that the sixties had it all—drama, flamboyance, style—while the seventies were more "privatized," preoccupied with the self. The phrases had already been minted. "The Me Decade," "the Culture of Narcissism." I could only laugh. I did not meet any women who had not been changed in the most fundamental ways by the decade. Yet, there they were, droning on about the dull seventies. They used convenient sixties symbols to make the point: Jerry Rubin was working on Wall Street; Tom Hayden (who had once been bailed out by a sister of Diana Oughton) was not only the husband of Jane Fonda and the father of one of her children, but was also running for office. See Dick, see Jane; see how we all grow old and settle down.

Not a single summary of the seventies that I saw spoke of the quiet revolution that was going on. Oh, there was a mention that women were entering the job market, as if *that* was new.

Yet Kathy was also very much a part of the seventies. A genuine radical with enormous energy, she could have been a thrilling leader of the feminist revolution. Why did she choose to pursue the violent macho idea of revolution instead?

I had some inklings, some hunches. For years my social and professional life overlapped that of the Boudins. I knew some of the more intimate aspects of their lives. I wondered if such familiarity would inhibit me. And the people who had first proposed the book wondered if the Boudins would cooperate and talk freely with me.

I waited a while before contacting them. It seemed that the last thing they needed was an intrusion from a writer, even a friend. But shortly after Brink's, pieces on Kathy started appearing everywhere. *People Magazine, The New Republic, The Nation, Win, Commentary, The Village Voice, Soho*

*Weekly News*; even *Mademoiselle* ran a piece on Kathy Boudin. But the one that broke my hesitation was a large cover story in *The New York Times Magazine* by Lucinda Franks, a Boudin family friend. The detail that stood out was a photo caption: "Leonard Boudin and his wife." I knew Jean as a writer who participated in a feminist writers' group. Yet to the media, Jean existed only as the wife of Leonard.

What about Jean? How was she now faring as mother of Kathy?

I got on the phone and called the Boudins. Jean answered. She told me she could not speak long; she was about to pick up Chesa, Kathy's thirteen-month-old son, and take him to visit his mother in jail. Then she added, "Do you know what it's like to be going on seventy and have the care of an infant child and your daughter on trial for murder?" Of course, I did not. I told Jean she sounded very strong, everything considered.

Jean Boudin at seventy is a beautiful woman. When Kathy was younger, she resembled her father. But now, at forty, she is older and more gaunt. Kathy's high cheekbones and deeply set clear, blue eyes make it evident that the resemblance is between mother and daughter. Only the ironic smile is the father's.

In the Bohemian circle of the Boudins, most of the men married striking women. Their arty get-ups, ethnic jewelry, and avoidance of ostentatiously feminine clothes prevented them from appearing like mere decorative appendages. And it wasn't only the big, looped earrings or the Guatemalan straw bag. The women not only looked artistic, they were artistic. Or more precisely, they had artistic aspirations. (Almost as important as striking looks was an ability to play an instrument, dabble at easel or notebook, and cook well.)

Of course, the women kept up with current affairs. They were attractive, talented, *and* informed. In other words, counterparts to their husbands. Except they did not have careers, or give speeches, or have dinners in their honor, or have visiting lectureships at prestigious universities, or get interviewed, or get recognized by their peers. They had no peers; they were wives. But not merely wives; wives of men highly respected in their fields. They kept the man's enterprise running behind the scenes, like the hands of a puppeteer. They made the home charming; they served the right meals with the right wines; they knew chic domesticity. To this day, I have never encountered the poorest Bohemian, one who lives in a style straight out of the Puccini opera, on the verge of selling his coat, who does not have the jug of wine and some nice old ceramic mug for home-ground, home-brewed coffee.

Because these women have lived in the shadows of their husbands, their contributions are rarely recognized. Even in homes where there are taste and charm and comfort, interior decor is relegated to a trivial hobby for rich, bored women. So, the wives of the Bohemian aristocrats rarely feel proud of their homes. Interior decor—yes, interior is the word—is frowned upon. It is not classy. It is crude, associated with six percenters, the equivalent of shyster lawyers, which the husbands of these women certainly were not.

Of course, the architecture—the exterior form of a home— is often commented upon; that is a chic calling, combining creative and mechanical talent with money. Forget the shelf lined with unusual dishes picked up from years of travel, brousing in curio shops while the man is presenting a paper or being honored somewhere; forget all the yard sales and garage sales in the country that have helped make the home a salon; that is what you "do" on vacation. Even the landscape gardener of the summer homes of the Bohemian aristocrats receives more respect for his work than the talented housewife.

Oh, her cooking is praised; she is said to be a good manager. And then one day she "breaks down" as the expression has it, and everyone pities her. The aristocrats send her off to the shrink. No one talks of it as a woman's way of going on strike, calling a halt to bad working conditions—no pay, no recognition, nothing the lowest worker takes for granted and the husbands fight for. Why, usually she does not even have a name, except "wife of."

Yet that is not unusual in the Boudin circle.

In 1968 I met Celia Gilbert, a poet living in Cambridge. She was never identified as a poet. She was either the daughter of I. F. Stone, whose wife is Jean Boudin's sister, or the wife of Wally Gilbert. When I first met Celia, Wally was a protege of James Watson. At a party in honor of Watson's book *The Double Helix,* being filmed for an ABC-TV documentary, everyone spoke of Wally's brilliance and said he would one day win a Nobel Prize. They were right; in 1980, Wally did. I heard of Celia's work through the women's literary journals that were just beginning to flower. No one, though, spoke as if Celia did anything on her own, although Celia went on to win the Emily Dickinson Poetry Prize.

Now, years later, I thought of what Celia had been through—when I met her and Wally, their young child was dying of leukemia. It was heartbreaking; yet I found Celia strong and talented. Despite personal tragedy, she was writing poetry.

Shortly after meeting Celia, I saw a documentary on her father. Although I had heard that her mother actually published *The I. F. Stone Newsletter,* a favorite in my own household, the movie, narrated by Tom Wicker, had just about nothing of her, Stone's wife. I think she appeared as a shadowy figure seen moving across a room while Izzy was shown meandering down the street mailing letters by hand, surrounded by hundreds of clippings in his jolly, one-man shop. Or reluctantly receiving an honorary something-or-other, while his wife, a Ph.D. in her own right, looked on.

It was clear Izzy loved his work; as he put it, "I should be in jail for having so much fun."

When I called Celia in Cambridge, she was as nice as I had remembered her, and it was with some awkwardness she said she did not feel free to talk about her aunt and uncle or their daughter. She said it had been a long time since she had seen Kathy, but she still remembered her clearly from their days as kids at Fire Island. Kathy was unusually talented as an athlete, and Celia could still see her running all over the place.

When Celia and her family no longer summered at Fire Island, they rented out their small bungalow. A friend of mine lived in it for one season; it was the time when many of the old Bohemian aristocrats were in transition. Nat Hentoff, a regular, had divorced and married Margot. Therapy—mostly Reichian—was popular with that crowd; so was jazz. Gerry Mulligan was said to have a cabin by the ocean called, in typical Fire Island parlance, Psycottage. Ocean Beach was a funky sort of town—relaxed, informal, good for kids—the summer vacation spot of many liberals in the mid-sixties. As most became better known and relatively affluent, they moved on to the Vineyard or the Hamptons. But there was a time when Joseph Heller, Nat Hentoff, I. F. Stone, and the Boudins all piled on the little ferry that crossed the Great South Bay and abandoned their cars and shoes to make do with little children's wagons for transportation, orgone boxes, jazz, gossip, and the ocean mist. It was a fine Bohemian playpen for adults and their children.

Besides the Fire Island memories, Celia recommended two articles: one by Ellen Cantarow in *Mademoiselle* and another by Midge Decter in *Commentary,* who repeated Lucinda

Franks' report of a statement attributed to Jean after the town house bombing.

According to Franks, Jean, unaware of Kathy's involvement in the fire, commented that firemen always put out the fires of the rich quickly. I doubt if Jean came up with such a simple-minded Leftist jingle. It would seem to me the honest response to learning that a very solid town house had burned down would be to wonder how it had happened, not how the rich get preferential treatment by the fire department. For as anyone who watches the news on TV knows, the fire department more often sends its truck to slums and risks the lives of its fire fighters to carry out poor people. Not because *poor* people get preferential treatment but because poor people live in housing that is more likely to burn or be burned. If Jean did feel compelled to make a social-justice type of statement, I suspect it was a desperate attempt to win her daughter's approval.

How it must have boomeranged! After all, the Boudins hardly live in a slum. For the Boudins had managed, in their choice of address, to have a beautiful brownstone bracketed by warehouses and rundown housing being transformed into trendy housing, thus introducing unintentional themes that were to play a part in Kathy's evolution—the theme of camouflage, of being borderline and hard to define, contradictory, on the cusp. Just the way Leonard achieved his fame as a lawyer—defending people who had broken the law on principle, like the Berrigan Brothers. But even as recently as 1981, about a decade after the Harrisburg Seven Trial, Philip, who was back in jail for some minor symbolic law breaking, slipped away (with official blessing) when his wife, the former nun whom he married after the trial, gave birth to their third child. Hence, another theme: the double standard of the liberal. One will go to jail on principle with the knowledge that one can leave for important occasions, such as the birth of a child. Most jailed people can't leave for any reason, as Kathy is now discovering.

My point is not that Berrigan shouldn't visit his child or that the Boudins should not live well. Merely that by projecting certain images, false (and naive) expectations are established. Although the Boudins live well, Leonard has never earned the kind of money he could have had he chosen wealth above all. But he is far from poor. Town houses, summer homes, seeing two kids through private school, Ivy League college and graduate school, frequent travels abroad, and tailored suits from Savile Row—these are the hallmarks of a certain class of Northeastern intellectual Leftists (except perhaps for Savile Row).

And, of course, that other hallmark—the wife is defined primarily by who her husband is.

I can still remember a large party given for a psychiatrist, active and well known in radical circles, and his wife, a painter. At the first meeting, the man, let us call him Tom Willis, a guru-type shrink, was the one you remembered. But once you got to know them you saw that were it not for his wife, we'll call her Lois Willis, he would not be able to function, even though he traveled the world, spoke on TV, lectured. As the sixties, his heyday, came to an end, and the seventies dawned, he started to spy on all-women's meetings. (This was on Cape Cod, where many of the Bohemian aristocrats summered.) He and his colleagues would crawl up to windows to hear what the women had to say at meetings that were closed to them.

Anyway, there was this party, and the phone rang. It was for him. It was very crowded and hard to hear; a group of us budding feminists (straight from previous capers such as pasting labels on subway posters saying, "This ad insults women") decided on a novel way to address him. We all, on cue, called out, "Lois Willis's husband!" And even when we went right up to Tom and yelled it in his ear, he did not respond. So strange was the form of address, he simply did not recognize it. When we finally, again on cue, called him by his actual name, he turned around instantly. For years, of course, Lois had been introduced as Tom Willis's wife.

A more painful memory is the memorial service for my father, a Bohemian aristocrat himself. The memorial, held in a charming brownstone, was given by his chamber music group and, aptly enough, fashioned after a sonata. There were three parts: the first, music; the second, informal and spontaneous reminiscence; and the third movement, back again to music, before adjoining for sherry in the charming backyard of the charming brownstone. It was the second "movement," traditionally the most moving, that hurt the most. I heard stories about my father that spanned close to half a century; they were not maudlin or sentimental. It was a form of oral history—various people recalled days when my father was first starting his bookstore, which was to become a popular meeting place for Leftists during the thirties. I listened to tales of his generosity, the gentle humor of people being reminded that fifty years later they still owed him the money he had agreed to lend for the only first edition of Grove's Music Dictionary.

I was proud of my father. But when I got up to speak, it was not about him. I spoke about how much he enjoyed coming home, after a trip to Cuba or Russia, say, and always having a tasteful home and home-baked pies, and the like. Without my mother's contributions (totally ignored, even though she was there and many who spoke had been the recipients of her graciousness), he probably would not have achieved many of the things he was being memorialized for.

And so I wasn't really surprised to discover a booklet with a photograph of a sophisticated, pensive Leonard Boudin on its cover, published when he was given the Tom Paine

Award. The booklet was prepared for the annual Bill of
Rights Day, a fund raiser dinner, of the National Emergency
Civil Liberties Committee. There were some articles, including ones by former students (Leonard, throughout his practice, had occasionally taken off a year to be a guest lecturer at
Harvard, Yale, Berkeley, or some other well-known university), who spoke of their awe of the man before they met him
and their respect for him afterward. The tone in these articles
was adulatory—Leonard was an idol. Most of the booklet
was taken up with small ads that honored Leonard, and, I
imagine, paid the cost of printing it. Many famous people
had sent in something, including almost every movie star
ever associated with liberal causes. There were also ads from
Leonard's family. His brother took out a space, and so did his
niece Ceilia, her husband, Wally, and their children. The
people in his office contributed a poem, in the spirit of a high
school yearbook, gently mocking Leonard's potential for
tyranny and vanity. Leonard was only human. Why, this
great defender of the oppressed actually has suits tailor-
made on Savile Row! If his colleagues were making fun of
Leonard, they were also making fun of themselves; it was all
right to tell jokes about the tribe within the tribe.

I had been told about the booklet by someone who went to
the dinner. I picked up a copy with hope it would provide easy
access to Leonard's bio. But I came away with something
more revealing than any single biographical fact. Of the
hundreds of commemorations—some light, some loving,
some serious—only one mentioned Jean. Jean, who was his
wife and companion, who was largely responsible for the
running of the Boudin salon and the family—first the blood,
then the surrogate children, and then the family of the Left. I
did not think the omission any more accidental than that of
my mother at my father's memorial "sonata." (Like Jean, my
mother had serious artistic aspirations; she had studied to be
a concert pianist at Juilliard.)

In fact, the entire booklet seemed more like a eulogy than praise for a person as alive as Leonard. The tone was adulatory. No one wanted to say a negative thing. One other entry stood out: it was to Leonard and mentioned his triumph over Ché in a game of chess. It was curious: the ad's signer, an attorney associated with Leftist causes, was a friend not only of Leonard's, but of Jean's. Why did she choose to ignore Jean? What kind of loyalty to Leonard blinded a woman of feminist sympathies?

Leonard is indeed a charmer. Bright, attractive, witty in a sardonic way, and successful, a combination that seems to go over big with a certain type of woman. Like his wife, the woman is striking looking; like the wife, she is talented; like his wife, she is up to date on world affairs. But she has one major difference. She is not a wife; she is a successful professional, usually a lawyer or a journalist.

I have known several young women whom Leonard has befriended. Besides the attributes I've mentioned, they have another, more subtle quality; they are vulnerable. They seem to be attracted to power. Power is magnetic, and they all are drawn to powerful men. Each of the women I knew longed for the right man—a powerful, successful, noble, public figure.

So it is not surprising that one admirer chose to express her feeling for Leonard by reminding him, and proclaiming, that he had beaten Ché, one of the world's most powerful Leftists, a man more myth than reality to most.

The Boudin brownstone has been home to many on the Left. There probably isn't a single activist from the sixties who doesn't at least know of Leonard Boudin.

Jean would have to wait till the seventies to be in circles where Leonard was not an idol to the many younger feminists who had never heard of him. Even if they had, Jean would never be known as Leonard's wife when she showed up for meetings of the Feminist Writers' Guild. At one of the earliest meetings of the New York City chapter, women had

175

gathered to discuss the policy of a new literary paper, *The Feminist Review*. Adrienne Rich, unable to attend, sent a letter to those of us present. She asked that we give particular attention to the works of women who are usually excluded by mainstream reviewing—minority women and lesbians. There was a lively discussion among the group, which was about half lesbian and half straight. The writers ranged from those as well known as Grace Paley, Alix Kates Shulman, and Andrea Dworkin to women who were still writing poems in their own rooms, women like Jean. (Ironically Jean would have to wait till 1983 when her daughter was about to be tried for murder to gain the recognition she deserved.)

The question arose whether a book by a man should ever be reviewed. The answer, everyone agreed, was no. Then came a question that elicited a more mixed response: should a capable man who was willing to give his time to editing and production be included? Most of the women were opposed. Jean stood up and argued for his inclusion, making the point that there were some men who were good and that the world couldn't exist if we excluded men. Although I disagreed with her and could hear the echoes of a life spent on the periphery of the male Left, eclipsed by its heroes (Leonard and his colleagues), I still admired her for having the confidence to state her views. I had heard, from a poet who took a course with Kenneth Koch in which Jean was also a student, that she was very shy and diffident and hardly ever spoke. So although I thought her point was a thinly disguised male apologist one, I liked looking at her blue eyes alive with excitement. In her orange parka, she fit in perfectly with the other fifty or so women, many of them part of Kathy's generation. And she seemed to enjoy the meeting.

Jean's participation stood out because I knew that a few hours on a Saturday afternoon, once a month, was a treat for her but an insignificant detail in the larger social/professional/political/artistic life she shared with Leonard. The

Boudin household is a "salon" frequented by famous men in many fields and their young admirers (there is nothing as magnetic to young people as high ideals). It was Lucinda Franks who described it that way in a story she wrote about Kathy for *The New York Times* after Brink's. When Franks wrote the piece, she was the wife of Robert Morgenthau, Manhattan District Attorney, although she was not identified that way. Only Jean was called the wife of . . . , anonymous to the person who wrote *The New York Times Magazine* photo caption.

Franks had shared a Pulitzer Prize for reporting on radicals of the sixties, in particular Diana Oughton. Although Morgenthau was roughly the same age as Leonard, his new wife, Lucinda, was younger than Kathy. I had seen them when they were courting, sitting inconspicuously in a restaurant that features reggae. That, too, fit in with the gestalt—powerful, older professional men involved with younger women with leftist sympathies.

Ben Spock was one who found a safe port at the Boudins'. Spock left his wife of many years for a woman roughly half his age and went into semiretirement, boating in the Caribbean or the waters near his solar home in Arkansas. He touched shore for select political occasions, briefing first Leonard and then Kathy (in jail) on the best way to deal with the separation from her son. Eventually it became known that the famous pediatrician's book, long the bible on child care and translated throughout the world, was written with the extensive help of his wife, although for a long time she did not receive credit.

Here is what she did, as stated by Spock when he credited her in a full page of his updated book in 1975. It is inscribed "To Jane with Gratitude and Love."

(1) Jane Spock typed the first draft from Ben's "slow dictation."

(2) She was responsible for such "details" as the recommended number of diapers, sheets, pads, nighties, shirts, bottles, and nipples and trying the formulas "to make sure they worked."

(3) While he was in the Navy, she consulted with specialists and publishers in New York, took down his changes by long distance telephone at two in the morning, and spent "hundreds of hours" on revisions and indexes.

(4) In short, "the book couldn't have been what it is without her."

For three years, not only did Jane help write the book that made Spock a medical, and later a radical, star, whom Leonard would defend, but she also was raising two sons. Still, she had no identity other than wife of . . .

My favorite response to finding out that Spock's wife played a major role in the book came from a young Hispanic mother who had a copy of the Spock book in Spanish. When I asked her if she knew that Spock's wife had written parts of it, she said she'd figured that. "How would anyone who doesn't stay home and take care of the kids know so much?"

Shortly after the Spocks' divorce, *The New York Times* sent a reporter to interview the former wife. She spoke of the loneliness after so many years of being married. I don't remember whether she mentioned the daily visits to the courtroom when Spock was on trial and Leonard was the attorney defending him. When in trouble, Ben Spock was able to present a portrait of devoted marital togetherness, the kind that comes across well to a jury.

Then there is William Kunstler, the most flamboyantly trendy, in radical chic terms, of all the stars of the leftist solar system. I used to enjoy watching him parade around Washington Square Village. Although he is now balding, his long gray hair blows forward so he looks like an aging balladeer. Kunstler, not to be outdone by the younger generation, took his place among the young mothers and a scattering of bearded young men. His new wife, a lawyer, was busy with her career.

Now the women were expected to have artistic professional ambition *and* to develop it. It was chic to be married to a woman of accomplishment, the way it had once been chic to be married to a woman who knew how to be the wife of a successful liberal professional.

But, in all fairness, the whole matter went beyond chic. The second wives were not only younger with fewer wrinkles and vaster sexual experience, but their careers gave them a confidence the first wives could never have. This confidence made them less dependent, and men—young and old—were discovering that being emotionally responsible for two (to say nothing of the financial burden) was less fulfilling than being emotionally responsible for yourself, even if it did entail a little less idolatry. Nevertheless, the sexual politics remain unchanged.

Why do I say that? Let me quote Kunstler himself. Before its demise, *The Soho Weekly News* ran a profile of Susan Tipograph, the defense attorney for suspect Judy Clark.

The profile discussed how the line between Tip's (as she is known) personal life and her political one is almost nonexistent. She lives the style of her clients and shares their views. She is not merely a detached professional who can twist the law to her client's advantage. She must also passionately believe her client is correct; she is concerned with right and wrong and uses the law as an instrument to further what she thinks is right and to destroy what she thinks is wrong. As Brink's suspects' lawyers, Tipograph and Kunstler are part of the same legal defense team. Kunstler has often spoken to the media of the unity of the defendants and their attorneys. (He issued such a statement when there was a real question about how the others would react to Samuel Brown after he gave information to FBI agents that led to further arrests.) Yet in this profile, Kunstler talks about Tip in terms that do

179

not suggest unity. "If you become so close to your clients that you become indistinguishable from them you lose effectiveness. You might as well become the client. Even though Susan's briefs are well reasoned, I can see where she'd hurt judges and D.A.'s because she's a tough cookie. You don't push Tip around."

A curious statement. Doesn't Kunstler admire tough cookies? His former client in the Brink's case, Anthony LaBorde, is a pretty tough cookie himself. Could it be that he admires only male tough cookies? Or is it that Tip's reputation as a radical lesbian is what really threatens Kunstler?

After all, what would the Boudin household look like at the dinner table if all the women were "tough cookies" like Tipograph? Well, for the time being, Kunstler and his cohorts do not have to worry; there still seem to be plenty of young, bright, attractive women who find power erotic.

Perhaps it was the daughters of the Left who had the problem of sorting through the double standard.

There is a theory about the origin of schizophrenia. It is called the *double bind* and goes something like this: A parent tells her/his child how much the child is loved. Yet the parent acts in an unloving and rejecting way. The child is confused. If the pattern is consistent, and if actual behavior constantly contradicts what is being said, the child begins to think that language does not have a shared meaning as the child had initially been taught. People say one thing but act in the opposite way. Therefore language doesn't have much function, except to confuse. In order to avoid confusion, the child slowly stops accepting the definition of words she/he was given and slowly begins to use language in a private way, eventually using utterances that have no meaning to anyone *except* the child. At least, she/he knows what it means and cannot be driven crazy by constantly having to sort through contradictions.

To live with a double bind—a split, a division, a contradiction, all the aspects of alienation that have been celebrated in contemporary literature (think of Camus's stranger who winds up performing a gratuitous killing), is to be a divided self. Probably the current fascination with aliens, for example, E.T. (a fascination that can also be observed with animals), is that one does not have to rely on verbal messages for communication. The nonverbal is more reliable, more intuitive, and will not betray its intended meaning.

Clearly Kathy was not an unloved or rejected child. Equally clearly, Kathy is not a schizophrenic. But I think that Kathy and other women of her generation who turned to violence as a means to change society were faced with a kind of schizophrenia in the culture of their parents' generation— a core of contradictions that represented a cultural condition analogous to what social scientists call a double bind.

I try to imagine what it is like for an extraordinarily intelligent woman to grow up watching her father deified by all sorts of people, his peers, beautiful young professional women to whom he could gracefully play the role of mentor, while Jean was nothing but wife of . . . , parroting her husband's ideas. How different from men in the country club set was Leonard's behavior? Was Jean's role any different from that of Patty Hearst's mother? What is one to do with this contradiction: One's father is known throughout Leftist circles for his high ideals as well as his charm and wit. Yet when it comes to women, his behavior is no different from that of any man regardless of his politics.

What is Kathy to make of the fact that one of his admirers, the surrogate son of sorts, quotes the father in a book about his famous trial, *The Harrisburg Seven,* as a man who says "I do not lose cases." And then is described as having a heart attack while dancing with four women at Fire Island and turning so blue that he looked like a derelict when he passed out.

Jean is described in the book as sitting in the front row of

181

the courtroom making sure that it was Valium Leonard was taking, not nitroglycerine by mistake. Here, in exaggerated form perhaps, is what Kathy witnessed all her life—an active father surrounded by worshipful young women and a passive mother sitting, worrying about her husband's health.

Kathy's opting for purity wasn't unusual. If the fifties held repression responsible for mental illness, the sixties insisted it was dishonesty that did you in. Hence, the insistence on authenticity, whether it be tribal dress, Afro hairdos, or names that respected roots. The point was to live consistently, to live as one believed, even if it meant sacrificing money, fame, and power. The ideal was noble, but hardly realistic.

There is no way a man can reach a top position in as high-status and high-pressure a profession as law without, at the very least, being at ease with power. But the Boudin philosophy does not allow for that. Nor does it allow for openly seeking power. Yet Leonard did, by defending heroes of the Left, star dissenters. What a double bind to those who claim to shun fame, let alone fortune.

I would suggest the core double bind for Kathy was the gap between the father's personal behavior and his idealistic politics. As a quick and sensitive child, she detected it at an early age. Kathy determined she would not speak one way and act another; she would be pure and uncompromising. She would not give in to what she felt she wanted but did not approve of; she would deny her feelings in order to avoid living with this contradiction.

Kathy must have incorporated the split inherent in liberalism—the easy identification with a people one knows nothing about, except in theory, in symbol, or in literary terms; her instincts were to deal with the real only, almost a simplistic reaction to abstraction. To take Leonard's high ideals one step further—not just to defend radical dissenters, but *to be one,* the most radical of all, a real revolutionary unafraid of

182

violence, prepared to do anything in the name of a cause—
The Revolution—she believed in.

What made Kathy worry so about the correct position,
about being judged wrong politically? So deeply patriarchal
a fear, some great white winner father might disapprove?
But alas, forgive.

That is what Leonard appears to have done. Kathy is his
daughter, his "darling" as a close family friend put it. Yet his
behavior as a professional, as a lawyer, provides certain
proof of my initial hunches—that the reputation of the male
Left was built on an inconsistency deeply rooted in the culture. An example: the change of venue motion filed by
Kathy's lawyers was based largely on the role of the press.
Attorneys for the New York Civil Liberties Union filed an
*amicus curae* brief. They see no inconsistency between
defending rights of Nazis to speak and pornographers to
publish, and seeking to limit, even silence, the press on behalf
of Kathy Boudin.

It is little wonder that Kathy sought refuge from contradiction with simple nurturing and direct experiences—organizing welfare mothers in Cleveland and then finally becoming
one herself while taking part in violent "revolutionary" acts.

It is almost as if the credo was: "It is extreme, therefore it is
real." So too, its flipside: "It is simple and ordinary, therefore
authentic." Hence, Kathy's lusting to become one with the
welfare mothers. But there is also the confusing contradiction of saying you care and then going home and living in a
way that would make you an alien to the people you say you
care about. For although Leonard did indeed defend dissenters, they were more like him than not; they were stars,
Leftist celebrities. In that respect, Kathy's stardom follows
quite logically. But Kathy took star dissension one step
further. She gave it real flesh and blood. What a pity she did
not follow Jean's wishes and become a doctor.

Having a child seems to have provided Kathy with the

183

experience of flesh. According to everyone, she is a devoted, loving mother. Her former roommate, Rita Jensen, said Kathy had gone shopping for a snowsuit at a flea market shortly before Brink's. Imagine what it must be like to go shopping for a snowsuit for your young son and then to go to a meeting where people are planning how to blow the brains out of the police if they are caught robbing a bank.

Rita Jensen spent a summer at a feminist camp, Sagarus. The women there remember her well. She fought to have male children in the community. One said, "I knew we'd be hearing about her in the future." I imagine that Kathy and she had a strong cooperative household, which makes Kathy's involvement with macho violence all the more puzzling.

Yet when all is said and done, Kathy remains alone. She is the only known Weatherwoman who did not surrender. She is the only fugitive who chose to remain one when all charges against her had been dropped. Something in her must have felt at home in the role of the alien, with aliases and the other paraphernalia of the underground life.

Even now, as she awaits her upcoming trial, she has managed to sever herself from all but one of her codefendants. What is most surprising for so devoted a mother is her seeming willingness to be on opposite sides politically and emotionally from codefendant David Gilbert, who is, after all, the father of her child.

But perhaps this is the only way Kathy can respond to the double message received from her father. Like most married men of his generation, Leftists, Rightists, or anything in between, Leonard believes strongly in the traditional family. Casual remarks made after the Brink's shootout reveal his traditional views. When speaking of the deaths, he referred to them as tragic because they left "widows and orphans." But they also left fathers and brothers and long-time companions. In fact, Mary La Porta, the person closest to Waverly at the time of his death, is left out of the picture entirely by such thinking.

I stated earlier that I think Kathy was reacting against a kind of schizophrenia in the culture of her parents' generation. I do not think she is alone. I think that the women who joined cults, who escaped into drugs and meditation, were reacting against it too. But they worked out less violent resolutions to the unbearable split they felt. Sally Kempton, a dozen years ago, wrote a memorable essay about her own experience. At the time, she was a journalist. Her father, Murray, was also a journalist and, like Leonard, was concerned with the oppressed (he wrote a perceptive book about the Panther 21 Case). Like Leonard, he is a witty sardonic man. Sally is very candid about how intellectually and spiritually seductive a father like that is for a bright young daughter. For her, the father established the pattern with men, the infatuation with older, powerful, protective figures whom she secretly wanted to bash over the head with a pot, especially after the relaxed meetings with her women's group where there was no need to impress, no need to win approval, no need to compete. She describes how being in such a group made her feel less sexual toward all men and more angry at her husband. But the reason she didn't bash him over the head or leave him (then) was simple: she was afraid. (Sally subsequently did leave him and went off to India to study meditation, living under another powerful man, this time one with a spiritual aura.) It is hard to kick the habit.

I think Kathy struggled with the same addiction—an attraction to power, a liking of high adventure, and an underlying longing for something real and fulfilling, which she seemed to find in a child.

I understand that feeling. Like Kathy Boudin and Judy Clark (and women everywhere, for that matter), I too had very much wanted a child, and as my reproductive years began to wane, I considered becoming a single parent. But short of becoming a welfare mother, there was no way I could swing it financially.

And so it was something of a miracle that when I moved to the country, the new place seemed to come with a young girl—almost nine at the time I moved in the summer of '81—just the age she would have been had I had a child when I could have easily borne her.

She lived down the driveway with her grandparents, who were raising her after she lost her mother when she was six. At first, we were a big sister/little sister duo. But by the end of the year, this child, *who was in no way of my womb,* had become the child I had always wanted.

I felt for Kathy, deprived of the flesh of her own child, who had come into the world dancing. The dance of life. But I wasn't about to let my feelings of maternal empathy allow me to forget that Kathy had chosen, with an ardor equal to the dance of life, the Big Dance—the dance of death. And for this contradictory choice she would have to be judged.

# NOTES AND ACKNOWLEDGMENTS

THE information in this book came from several sources.

For the dramatization in Part I, Hal Davis, a court reporter for the *New York Post,* and I retraced the events as closely as possible. Our recreation of them is based on our findings and the extensive coverage of *The Journal-News.* But it was not only the thoroughness of the reportage that enabled us to retrace the crime scenario; it was also the careful unbiased reporting of the Brink's story, which also earned the paper an award from the New York State Associated Press. I would like to credit staff writer John Castelluci, in particular, for his in-depth and original investigative reports as well as his superb day-to-day coverage.

The staff members of the Nyack Public Library were generous with their time in helping me track down back issues of *The Journal-News* and make copies of relevant material.

The copies led Hal and me to "Mary La Porta, the girl friend of Waverly Brown." While reams of print kept pouring out about the Brink's tragedy, Mary provided a human dimension. Throughout this project, she shared her pain, her anger, her desire to understand, and gave me an idea of what it's like to be the innocent survivor of a murder victim.

At the Pickwick Book Shop in Nyack, I came across *Rediscovering the Nyacks: Village Guides, Walking Tours.* They helped us locate Mary's apartment, retrace the route of the crime, and enabled us to become familiar with Nyack in general. *South Nyack Centennial, 1878-1978,* gave me a sense of the village's history. This booklet was also purchased at Pickwick, whose proprietor, John Dunnigan, was kind (and trusting) enough to lend me his sole "collector's edition" of *The Bust Book,* printed by Grove Press in 1969, and coauthored by Kathy Boudin.

Kathy's prison observations are part of the public record and are on file in the Manhattan Federal Court.

In Nyack's used book store, I purchased *SDS* by Kirkpatrick Sale (Random House, 1973), which provided some useful details in the background section of Part II.

However, most of the information about Kathy's political life in the '60s was taken from Thomas Powers's *Diana: The Making of a Terrorist* (Houghton Mifflin Co., 1971).

William O'Rourke's *The Harrisburg 7 and the New Catholic Left* (Thomas Y. Crowell Co., 1973) shed light on Leonard and his relation to Kathy.

The following passage in Gail Godwin's novel, *A Mother and Two Daughters* (Viking Press, 1982) provided further insight into a father-daughter relationship:

> In some ways, Cate had done as he would have liked to do, had he been less prudent, more furious and full of fire. Perhaps it was wrong in him, but he did look forward, with anxious eagerness, to whatever his older daughter might decide to do next. Not that he wished her any danger; or rather, not any danger that his prudence and foresight couldn't get her out of.

Jane Alpert's *Growing Up Underground* (William Morrow, 1981) was revealing about Kathy as a woman as was David Behrens's interview of Alpert, published in *Newsday,* October 29, 1981.

The following articles, listed chronologically, were, in varying degrees, useful:

"Cutting Loose" by Sally Kempton (*Esquire,* July 1970 and reprinted June '83 in the fiftieth anniversary issue)

"Separating Terror from Radicalism" by Sheldon Wolin, (Op-Ed, *The New York Times,* 11/3/81)

"A Change in the Weather" by Paul Berman (*Village Voice,* 10/28/81)

"Boudin: Girl on the Run" by Eric Nadler (*Soho Weekly News,* 11/3/81)

and

"The Road to Nyack" (*Soho Weekly News,* 11/3/81)

"The Seeds of Terror: How Children of Privilege Became the Weather Underground" by Lucinda Franks (*The New York Times Magazine,* 11/22/81)

"Women of the Weather Movement" by Gabrielle Burton ("Letters" of *New York Times Magazine,* 1/10/82)

"White Heat Underground" by Todd Gitlin (*The Nation,* 12/19/81)

"The End of the Seventies" by Peter Shaw (*The New Republic,* 12/23/81)

"Inside a Radical Group" (*Newsday,* 1/10/82)

"Notes From the American Underground" by Midge Decter (*Commentary,* 1/82)

"Behind the Brink's Case" by M. A. Farber (*The New York Times,* 2/16/82)

"Kathy Boudin: Days of Rage, Nights of Anguish" by Ellen Cantarow (*Mademoiselle,* 2/82)

"'Tip' of the Brink's Case" by Ralph Gardner, Jr. *(The Soho Weekly News,* 3/2/82)

"The Untold Story of the Weather Underground" by Peter Collier and David Horowitz (*Rolling Stone,* 9/30/82)

"Putting Juries on the Couch" by Morton Hunt (*The New York Times Magazine,* 11/28/82)

In addition to John Castellucci and *The Journal-News,* I'd
like to single out one other reporter and paper. As far as I
know, Jill Nelson was the only reporter to interview Samuel
Brown and call attention to his role as a man caught in the
middle. *The Village Voice,* which printed the interview on
May 4, 1982, did so before Brown was thought newsworthy
by any other news-gathering organization.

"Liberation in Our Lifetime: A Call to Build a Revolutionary Anti-Imperialist Women's Liberation Movement," a
pamphlet written by the members of the May 19th Communist Organization, provided direct information about their
political ideology.

The booklet, "poems by women of the weather underground," gave me some insights into their feelings.

"The Bill of Rights Journal" published by the National
Emergency Civil Liberties Committee devoted its December
1979 issue to Leonard Boudin and, in so doing, added to my
understanding of Leonard's professional and personal
status.

The following radio interviews gave me a fuller picture of
Jean:

"Senior Edition," May 31, 1983, WNYC/FM
"Casper Citron," June 2, 1983, WQXR AM and FM

Now to individuals.

Hal Davis helped me recreate the events in the first part of
the book; he also explained the ins and outs of the legal
labyrinth that Kathy had led herself into. His friendship and
support were as important as his reportorial and writerly
talents.

Desmond Smith of the Canadian Broadcasting Corpora-
tion who frequently writes on media, read the manuscript at
an early stage. With a cinematic eye and a writer's ear, he

gave me invaluable suggestions for revision. So did editor and friend Joy Johannessen.

Poet Jane Augustine and poet/critic Michael Heller shared their reactions with the honesty and sensitivity of fine writers and intelligent critics.

For the past five years, I have had a friendship through letters with Bill Gottlieb. It started when he was 88 and is still going strong. I want to thank Bill for keeping me in writing shape with his rigorous weekly workouts in words. Also Bill read every version of this book and, with each one, commented on whether I had kept sight of the main subject: Kathy Boudin. Without his feedback, the focus might have been less sharp.

Julie Coopersmith, agent, and Carol Calhoun, attorney, each did a remarkable job as professionals and dear friends.

Sol Stein had the courage to consider this manuscript and Patricia Day the enthusiasm that led to its acquisition. She also chose to edit it. With singular talent, Stein and Day transformed it into a book in record time.

No book comes to be without a typist. Mary Ann Gauger, a freelancer in Sag Harbor, made me glad I don't have a word processor. As with previous works, she was there to type, paste, patch, and give a human response to each new version of the book. She, too, worked in record time.

Many political women discussed with me the Brink's case and Kathy Boudin, in particular. They provided insights and information. To name them here might be against their wishes.

Political is also personal. I wrote this book while living in a country compound with my mate, a man. All the other members were women. With their support, their trust, they welcomed me, and without ideology or slogans we became a close community.

# KATHY BOUDIN AND THE DANCE OF DEATH

Women have supported me financially as well. I gratefully acknowledge the grant provided by the Money for Women Fund, Inc. The fund was founded by Barbara Deming, a longtime poet, pacifist, feminist lesbian. For years, her work has influenced my political thinking. But her words began to hold a deeper meaning for me as I thought about Kathy Boudin's involvement in a male-dominated, violent "revolutionary" group. And writing about Kathy in a gentle all women's community gave the following passage from *Remembering Who We Are,* Pagoda Publications, 1981, a special relevance.

> If we do make it [the identification between women, gay and straight] we can at last put from us the fear that has disabled us for so long: the fear that it is not for us to invent ourselves, the fear that men have the right to tell us whether we are real women or not real women. . . . We will be free at last—to both give and receive—because no one will be mothered as a god who overwhelms the motherer, presumes to be the motherer's only reason for being. All of us will be content at last to be simply human (it is enough) . . .

AUTHOR'S NOTE

On September 3, 1983, the jury in the five-months Federal Brink's trial held in Manhattan handed down a mixed verdict. All six defendants were acquitted of robberies involving murders. Sekou Odinga (formerly Nathaniel Burns) and Silvia Baraldini were found guilty of conspiracy and racketeering: each charge carries a sentence of up to 20 years. Edward L. Joseph and Cecil Ferguson were found guilty of having hidden a suspect after the Brink's robbery. This accessory charge carries a maximum of twelve and one-half years. Bilal Sunni-Ali (formerly William Johnson), charged with a Bronx robbery in which a guard was killed, was acquitted and released, as was Iliana Robinson, who was charged with helping two suspects escape.